DEE NORTHCUTT

# ROADMAP FOR LIFE

A Guide to Mindset, a Practice,
and a 15-Year Sprint to a Life of Wealth

Roadmap to Wealth Series LLC
© 2024 by Dee Northcutt
All rights reserved. No part of this publication may be reproduced, stored in a retrieval system, or transmitted in any form or by any means, including electronic, mechanical photocopying, recording, or otherwise, without the prior permission of Roadmap to Wealth Series LLC—except in the case of brief quotations embodied in critical reviews and certain other noncommercial uses permitted by copyright.

Printed in the United States of America
10 9 8 7 6 5 4 3 2 1

ISBN: 979-8-9904508-2-0 (paperback)
ISBN: 979-8-9904508-0-6 (hardcover)
ISBN: 979-8-9904508-4-4 (e-book)

Edited and Proofread by Kristina Paider
Cover and Book Design by Choi Messer

# CONTENTS

**DEDICATION** .................................................................. v
**INTRODUCTION** ............................................................. 1

**PART 1: CONVENTION**

    **Chapter 1:** Get Schooled: Breaking Convention ............. 13

    **Chapter 2:** The Conventional Timeline is All Wrong ........ 27

    **Chapter 3:** My Recipe ............................................ 41

**PART 2: LEARN THE KEY LESSONS OF WEALTH BUILDING**

    **Chapter 4:** The 5 Wealths ....................................... 57

    **Chapter 5:** SMART Goals + Smarter Plans .................. 73

    **Chapter 6:** The Psychology of Mindset: Abundance vs Scarcity ......................................................... 91

    **Chapter 7:** Productive, Consumptive, Destructive—How You Use Your Time .................................................. 103

**PART 3: APPLY IT TO LIFE**

    **Chapter 8:** Enjoyment ........................................... 119

    **Chapter 9:** Guidance for Different Life Stages .............. 131

    **Chapter 10:** Dad Rant ............................................ 143

    **Chapter 11:** Dream Schedule: Investing Your Time ......... 153

    **Chapter 12:** Sample Goals, Plans, Budgets + Reverse Budgets ................................................................. 163

    **Chapter 13:** What I Would Do Now If I Were You .......... 181

## IV  ROADMAP FOR LIFE

**Chapter 14:** Applying the 5 Wealths in Your Teens & Early 20s .................................................................... 195
**SUMMARY** ................................................................... 203
**EPILOGUE** ................................................................... 207
**ABOUT THE AUTHOR** ................................................. 213

#  DEDICATION

To Sara, you have played and continue to play a very important part in our success. You are one of a kind (intelligent and driven, a beautiful person inside and out, with the greatest personality). You have a stringent workout regimen, and it shows. You work hard to keep our family's needs satisfied. I have always been amazed at how you work hard, work out hard, and then still have time to perform all of the jobs that a mom and wife do to make life easy for a family. It has been said many times that being a stay-at-home mom is a full-time job. You have been able to have a successful professional career while being the best and most successful at doing all "stay-at-home mom" jobs. You are also the foundation of our great relationship. I could go on but will simply say thanks for being my life partner and best friend.

To RT and B, I wrote this book in a series of books for you to get a better understanding of me and my thinking while teaching you the cliff notes of what I've learned through both my traditional and self-directed education, with a heavy dose of my personal perspective. My hope is to inspire you to do more, dream big, and live the wealthiest life that can be attained.

I hope you will view me as a tough parent who guided you down the right path, loved you, and became your greatest friend and mentor as you transitioned into adulthood and for the rest of your life.

I will provide some insight into things that I have gotten right, and also totally failed at, with the intention of helping you get a head-start in life. In these pages, I will show you what I'd do the same and what I'd do differently if I could have a do-over. It is not to tell you how to live your life.

To all readers, I originally wrote this just for my kids. As a family, we thought others may learn and benefit from this, too. We thought, maybe it's the financial guidance and conversation we all wish our father had with us when we were in our late teens or early 20s, or even beyond that. I have kept the original tone and voice directly talking to my kids totally candidly, with no filters. I invite you to imagine you are at our kitchen table, listening in on our conversation.

Please note, in no way do I think my way is the only way, but my language is at times, direct. Feel free to take what applies or resonates with you and leave the rest behind. My goal is to share my authentic journey from my early 20s with $300k in debt to my early 40s and financially free (and by that, I mean very financially free) and am now on the path to $300M with an ultimate goal of $1B in wealth.

Whatever your age or stage of life, whatever your gender, race, or identity, this book is for everyone. Welcome.

# 📍 INTRODUCTION

I USED TO JOKE THAT I read only one book before I was 25. Sad. But true.

I struggled in school from day one. I always felt behind. I never felt like being a good student (at anything) was possible for me. Frankly, the construct of the school itself seemed largely like a waste of time.

What changed? It was not a lightning bolt of inspiration or a teacher who spent extra time with me (my mom tried, it didn't work), or a magical moment where the angels wept and the choirs sang and the heavens opened. Rather, it was a circuit breaker box that needed to be relocated. More specifically, it was me not having the money to pay an electrician and the desperate need and desire to do it myself.

Mom and I bought a fixer-upper. We were committed to remodeling it the way we wanted, so that meant a new kitchen and converting the garage into a primary bedroom. To do that, we had to update the plumbing and install new electricity, which meant moving the circuit breaker box. Really almost everything one would do in a complete renovation or addition.

I could do the basics, but I needed much more knowledge to understand things like structural load for taking out walls, advanced electrical and plumbing, and other big-ticket remodel items. So there I was, caught between a book and a hard place—the hard place being a contractor we could not afford. I went to The Home Depot and grabbed three thick "how to" hardcover books.

And the story of me versus the circuit breaker box, I become victorious. That's where I made friends with reading.

## HARD WORK FROM THE GET-GO

MY FAMILY WAS A TRADITIONAL middle-class family. Both of my parents worked hard: my mother was a teacher and librarian, and my father was a utility company employee. I was taught from a young age that I had to put in long hours to make a good living. My parents left the house at 5:30-6 in the morning and got home at 5:30 or 6 in the evening.

Our middle school playground led to our grandparents' backyard. Mamaw and Papaw would watch us after school. Papaw was a hard worker, and they both had multiple jobs and side hustles to make ends meet. When I was eight or so, Papaw taught me how to trap and fish, as he sold fish and furs. He also sold vegetables from the garden at a local farmer's market. He was always active.

As a teen, I was like Papaw in many ways. I liked to do different things and I liked to be busy. Papaw and I would go hunting and fishing often. He also taught me how to scale fish and skin animals. He was an intriguing person to be around. One of my favorite side trips was going to the grocery store with Papaw and my brother. He'd ask for 2 small one-pound paper sacks and he'd tell us to fill 'em with candy. So we loved going with him.

There was always something interesting to do. My grandparents always got by with different, smaller jobs, and were always busy with their hands.

They took care of all of us kids, plus our great-grandmother, who was frail and needed full-time care. And even with all that work, all the hunting, fishing, and gardening, they barely made ends meet. I don't think it ever occurred to them to have great-grandma in a facility. It wasn't an option.

## I WANTED MORE—AND DIFFERENT, AND YOU PROBABLY DO, TOO

AS A TEENAGER, I WORKED between two and four jobs, just like Papaw—bussing tables in a restaurant, cashier at a gas station, mowing and landscaping at a church, working on a line in a print factory, monitoring cardiac telemetry in a hospital, couriering for a bank, and TV production for a pilot high school TV class, plus construction work. This was in addition to yard work and chores required of me at home. I also woke many mornings when not working or when school was out to go hunting or fishing.

So, my work ethic and initiative were ingrained in me.

I quickly learned that I did not want to work any of these jobs long-term. I got bored doing the same thing at a job day in and day out.

Additionally, I realized that I wanted to make much more money than I could at any of the types of jobs I had in high school and most of the jobs that my parents and all those around me were making. The biggest realization that I had at a pretty young age was noticing how the middle-class people around me lived at retirement age and in their later years.

But I can tell you that seeing how hard and repetitive it was to work at a factory, working double shifts, working night shifts, and just seeing adults who worked these jobs their entire lives had a huge impact on my appetite for not wanting to do those jobs as an adult.

And then the real hammer came down. Mamaw and Papaw, who had lived a good, long, active life, had to go into a nursing home. It seemed more like a prison. They went from being always busy to just lying in a bed that was electronically raised and lowered. It was like low-income housing with not a lot of service. They were in bed full time. Someone checked on them twice a day. They'd raise the beds to talk to us, but otherwise, they didn't move. In addition, they were financially helpless.

Papaw went in first, and then Mamaw followed six months later. She passed first, and he shortly after. Their rapid decline hit me hard. It was very disturbing to me.

This experience led me to an unusual obsession at a young age (17-22 years old): this is not how I want my life to be—I do not want to retire and live out the final days of my life the way most around me were living. I did not want to be dependent on others in the form of a retirement home, social security, or becoming a burden on my family. I was a bit different from other kids my age because this was my worry.

I was distraught over my grandparents. I never wanted that for myself, and began to wonder, "Why don't I just take that whole piece out? Why don't I work to *not* get to that stage?"

I believe that this set a foundation and gave me the thought and drive I needed to invest in my later life from the beginning of my adult life. So, my understanding of long-term thinking and planning helped me to overcome the instant gratification mindset that much of our society has embraced.

## MY GOAL FOR AGE 65 REACHED 20 YEARS EARLY

IT WAS NOT THAT I was smarter or better than anyone else, but instead, I was so frightened of living my life from age 65 to 85 in a poverty state, that I forced myself to think long-term—well, accidentally. This long-term thinking is what has been the underlying guide for me to do all the things that I do and discuss in this book. Not only was I thinking long-term, but I was ultra-focused on this goal.

As I reached my early forties, I achieved the financial freedom that I set out to reach by age 65. As a result, I've been able to pivot and use those same goals, plans, and mindset to forge a path of leaving a legacy for my family generations after me. A legacy of financial freedom and hopefully a different way of viewing the world around me.

With my somewhat non-traditional success and how I've raised you kids, I have new concerns about how to ensure that you understand the importance of these qualities and mindsets so that you build on this legacy instead of taking it for granted and losing all that has been and will be provided to you.

## THE MOST IMPORTANT TAKEAWAY

THE MOST IMPORTANT TAKEAWAY is very simple. Wealth IS NOT being rich, it's not how much money you have, your status, others' perception of you, or others' perception of your life. Wealth is a mindset and a practice—all five aspects of it. More to come in Chapter 4.

If I give you $10,000,000 and you do not understand that wealth is a mindset and the philosophy behind it, then you will lose that money in a matter of months or years and be broke. Wealth is a mindset and a practice.

We've seen this happen with professional athletes, actors, music artists, and other celebrities all the time. We've also learned that inheritances are usually lost by the third generation. The "shirtsleeves to shirtsleeves in three generations" adage, which describes the inability of grandchildren to manage the wealth passed down to them from their grandparents and parents threatens the continuation of family legacies.

This is because there was never an understanding of the philosophy behind wealth. If I had a choice to give you an understanding of true wealth and the philosophy behind it or to give you $10,000,000, I would give you $0 and provide the understanding of wealth every time.

Wealth is a mindset and a practice—a way of thinking and understanding. My greatest wish for you is to understand this wealth mindset and to be able to teach and pass down this wealth to your children, them to their children, and so on. This is the only way that we can build a true family legacy and transfer financial wealth down generationally.

I know that working as a teen made it easy for me to work hard right out of college. I worry that my and your mom's success and getting to a point where we did not have to work hard as you were growing up will make it harder for you to have a strong work ethic.

Based on what I've seen of my peers, being a child in a financially wealthy household more often than not results in kids who lack motivation and drive as adults. I will say however, that I believe that the bulk of those kids did not have any direction from their parents and did not have any books written for them to explain the importance of a strong work ethic, setting goals, planning, and being successful.

To back up a bit, Mom and I had pretty much retired at ages 40 and 41. I actually used to say I retired at age 28 to be a stay-at-home dad, but then went back to work at age 30 and retired again at age 41 and have been retired ever since. Granted, I was driven by the fear of poverty and motivated by a deep desire for a better life.

On any given day—or almost every day—you'd leave for school at 7:30 to see me heading off to work out or doing something around the house in a t-shirt and shorts. You would later come home from school at 3:00 pm to see me sitting in a recliner and watching TV. Of course, you might not have realized that I was not actively watching TV, but instead had it as background noise as I worked on my laptop.

In contrast, I saw my parents leave for work as early as 5 am and return between 5 and 6:30 pm five days a week, while you saw two stay-at-home parents who looked as though they were living Saturdays every day of the week. And to be honest, we are living Saturdays seven days a week because we have retired and are doing work that we actually love.

Giving you this background is also a way for me to provide you with an example or roadmap for transitioning from a consumptive teen to a successful, wealthy, and productive adult. Playing the long game is the way to be successful—it's part of the wealth mindset and practice, as you will see in the pages ahead.

## MY SOLUTION TO GETTING MORE

MY SOLUTION TO GETTING MORE, sooner, is, in essence, developing your wealth mindset, a practice, and a very focused, planned 15-year work sprint. Ideally, you do the sprint from your mid-twenties to your early 40s, but realistically it can be started in your 50s, 60s, and beyond. I have found in myself and others, what this push in the earlier years can do to your foundational wealth. Namely, it sets you on a trajectory for maximum enjoyment and wealth, in alignment with your highest energy and drive in that period of your life.

Why those years? Because you have the most physical energy and drive. Can you start earlier or later? Absolutely. Way later, like at 60? Absolutely. Why start in your early twenties? Because you've had time to prepare, experiment, win, lose, recover, and elevate in that time, and you can choose a direction that is interesting and compelling to you, even if it's not your exact end-game. Why 15 years? Because that's about the time it takes to build and layer your success. Do you like the idea of retiring in your 40s (or in the next 15 years, wherever you're at) with more satisfaction, fun, and doing what you want? Read on.

# PART 1
## Break Convention

# GET SCHOOLED: BREAKING CONVENTION

I WAS THE LAST KID to read in my first-grade class.

I vividly remember studying with my mom for a spelling test and I just could not get it. It had to be painstakingly hard for her to have the patience to sit and try to help me. I would roll around on the floor, not wanting to be there. She would try to get me to focus on the next word, and I just couldn't do it. Looking back, I'm sure I had undiagnosed attention deficit disorder or a learning disability. From there forward, I was always on the lower levels of books and reading—I never made up that ground.

Later in school, I struggled with addition, subtraction, and multiplication tables. They were tough for me. I've always felt that getting behind early kept me from getting to be an A student. I also always felt like I spent hours studying with very little to show for it. In college, I would sit in my room studying much more than my roommates, but I just could not focus and let the knowledge sink in. I did not let this slow me down, but it probably gave me more drive to work hard to be successful. In fact, many successful people were not the greatest book-smart people.

Between my learning challenges and the devastation I felt witnessing my extremely active grandparents' rapid health decline in poverty, I look at life differently than 99% of the people in our world.

## THE RIGID CONVENTION

THE GOVERNMENT SAYS THAT YOU must attend school for twelve years—not your right—but the law—and then shames you into at least four more years of education at college. Parents have been programmed to go along with this need for kids to get good grades in subjects that will have little use for those kids in adulthood.

Education is more about government control than your actual needs. I'm not saying you should quit school or tell your friends that they and their parents are idiots for following these archaic rules. School does offer some basics that are helpful in life. More importantly, school provides a place to socialize and engage in group activities such as sports, theater, band, etc. But parents then say you need good grades to get into college. Alone this statement is fine. However, they want their kids to go to college and get good grades so that they can then work hard for the rest of their lives, which is the beginning of things going downhill.

If we are passive about thinking about what we want and setting our own goals and horizons, we will be pushed, pulled, and shaped by society. I don't want that for you. Rather, I want you to actively consider what you want out of life and do what you want to do. I want you to have fun.

I eventually graduated with a BA degree. Eventually, because I left school six credits shy of a diploma, worked for five years, and ultimately went back to get the piece of paper. So I barely graduated college five years after I should have.

I've rarely if ever used anything I learned in college. In my opinion, far more can be learned with on-the-job training. Those who apprenticed under a mentor could do much better than someone with a degree in the subject. Acknowledging that I have a complete bias, I think the institution and convention of education needs disruption.

Most of the things that are taught in school quite honestly have no bearing on our lives and our success. For many, it forms this opinion and feeling of dread or even hate toward the thought of education, as it did for me. On the other hand, knowledge that we elect and self-direct outside of the traditional experience can provide wealth with no bounds.

We thrive and succeed in areas of our lives that we find commonality and enjoyment. Someone or a school forcing us to learn is much different than us deciding on our own that we want to learn and be good at something.

Higher education has become an industrial complex, driven by a high-ticket marketing machine. Additionally, in some places, the government has turned primary school into this pre-socialist type of scenario that has really taken education in the wrong direction in my opinion.

The best lessons from early education and college play a role in learning to form relationships, transition from dependency to independence, learning to be goal-oriented in sports, and a few other positive aspects. School and especially college are breeding grounds for important social aspects. Therefore, I am still a proponent of school and college, but wish that they were functioning and running in a different capacity.

## LEARN HOW TO BE A GOOD EMPLOYEE

More importantly, personal education after school and/or college is the only way to true educational wealth. In my mind, school and college today teach us how to be a good follower and a good employee who works for "the man." If you find something in life that you enjoy and can make money at, then you will want to succeed in that job. You will search out and want to find education to help you grow in that position.

I would advise you to work for yourself and not for someone else, in order to have the freedom of time and have no ceiling on growth. I do understand that most of our society does not think this way and you may be of the opinion of that group of people that prefer to work for someone or a company. There is nothing wrong with either, but it is more important to find your fit where you achieve joy in your work. You will learn more in one year of working than you learn in sixteen years of school and college. Nothing beats on-the-job training.

The outdated and antiquated systems and requirements of schools and colleges are not what our society needs them to be. For example, very few of us will need to know how to graph a sine or cosine. Additionally, our public schools have gotten into assessment testing for funding, which has nothing to do with proper learning. It is not enough to know the answer, but you have to provide a specific path in which the correct answer was learned. Who cares how you get the correct answer if the answer is correct?

Now there are so many things wrong with public schools and things that have been both added and taken away from the curriculum. This is obviously my personal opinion. A basic understanding of subjects is necessary, but so many of the additional teachings are unnecessary. Additionally, on-the-job training could have a much more profound effect than some school teachings. Consider a medical or dental doctor—they still do an apprenticeship. It is called doing clinics or internships, but they are fundamentally apprenticeships.

There are some basics in specific majors that might help, but I feel that the bad info that must be retrained in real-world work might outweigh any basics learned, especially for entrepreneurs or those going into real estate investing. American entrepreneur and author Robert Kiyosaki says that schools teach kids how to work for someone else. I 100% agree.

There are professions that require degrees, such as attorneys, physicians, accountants, and the like, and if you want to be in one of those professions, go for it. You will still be working for someone. A small percentage will end up owning their own business, but most will work for someone for at least some period of time. Again, not to say anything is wrong with working for someone, but instead highlighting the fact that school and college are society's way of teaching students how to work for someone else.

College plays an important role in helping one grow in these ways:

1) getting away from home and becoming independent with some structure in place (requirement of being in classes).
2) and most importantly, socializing and making great contacts for personal and business growth in the future.

Now, as an employer, seeing your good or passing grades from high school and college mainly gives me an understanding that the job applicant is capable of getting a job done, has initiative, and has the drive. People who struggle in school and college could also have these same qualities. They just might have to prove even more that they have the drive, initiative, and ability. Those might also have to show more persistence than others.

I prefer an applicant with social skills, integrity, drive, initiative, and persistence over a high-grade student who lacks one or more of these qualities. There is also a third group of people that possess higher grades along with social skills, integrity, drive, initiative, and persistence.

Consider that only 27% of college graduates work in a field related to their degree. This statistic alone should show the relevance of college classes and grades, outside of showing capability. I would go so far as to say that most do not have a true grasp on what they are passionate about and what field they would most enjoy by the time they graduate college, much less when applying for college.

Due to this fact, I would suggest a business degree, for the two of you, if any diploma at all. I would get the minimal hours necessary for the degree. I would also try to get classes that I would be able to get the most out of (those with real-world applications). Learning a second language may be more applicable in business than calculus. At the same time, technology will handle translations for us in the future.

Educators in colleges tend to look down on the Greek system. I would argue that it was just as valuable, if not more valuable than classes. I was forced to learn more social skills. I made connections. I also figured out how to balance work and play. College and Greek life only magnify and speed up the pass/fail part of college, due to many failing to be able to balance between work (classes) and play (Greek life).

If I had it to do over again or if there was something I could have done better, it would have been to make more connections and cultivate more relationships. With social media, this can take on such a different dynamic and present more possibilities.

Of course, there still needs to be a balance between building connections and relationships with the education, learning, and understanding of one's self. Becoming a social butterfly alone will not get one a job. Balance is important here.

## THE DRIVE TO PROVE MY WORTH

As for me, I was not a good student in grade school, high school or college, so I am biased. As I began college, I decided that I wanted to work toward attending optometry school and become an optometrist. I was not accepted into optometry school due to my GPA being too low. I have no doubt that in the actual optometry business, I would have been in the top 1% of all optometrists if I had gotten in and graduated from optometry school.

Looking back, I'm so glad that I did not get in. It might have held me back from the great success that I am currently experiencing. I enjoy making my own hours and employing doctors instead of being a doctor, keeping regular business hours, and seeing patients on a regular schedule.

Doing poorly in school gave me the drive to want to prove my worth and that I could do better than those who did really well in school. School at all levels teaches us to be good workers. Better grades meant that one could get paid more by an employer. Fortunately for me, this forced me to think about ways to make more money outside of being an employee, which only left me with the path of being an owner/employer/entrepreneur.

Falling into this situation accidentally was luck, but it showed me the realization that unfortunately society and higher education sell to kids and their parents that those with good grades can get a good job. This virtually assures that any kid who gets good grades is destined to be an employee. Do not misunderstand me; I'm not saying that being an employee is bad. Being an employee is a great thing for many people. It just wasn't my path. And knowing you, I don't think it's yours.

Kids are often pushed by parents and their community down the route of being an employee because of school, grades, convention, and the perceived risk of being an entrepreneur or business owner. Generally, without actively thinking about, fully analyzing, or considering that we want something and setting our own goals, we are pushed and pulled in the direction that life takes us. I want to ensure that you actively consider what you want out of life and make the decision to become who you want to become.

With regards to financial wealth, this means that you decide and set goals to be an employee or owner/entrepreneur. Either path is great, but the mistake is letting society determine your path instead of taking control and making an informed decision.

## IT'S CALLED WORK FOR A REASON

"IT'S CALLED WORK FOR A reason," they say. Not in my book!

Some will say, to find a job you enjoy while others will say to find something that you are passionate about. Those who don't think work should be fun are simply put, not going to be truly wealthy. They may be successful and financially wealthy, but they will not be wealthy in all aspects of life.

I believe you must enjoy and be passionate about what you are doing in life to get the most out of it. I also believe that a job or how one makes a living is a huge part of their daily life. This is what multi-millionaire entrepreneur and author Garrett

Gunderson calls "soul" purpose and what we should truly be striving to figure out and understand.

Those who really achieve great success in business or in a job are working within their soul purpose. They are passionate about what they do. They enjoy what they get to do daily. These people cannot find enough hours in the day compared to those prodding and trudging through a job who cannot get the hours and minutes of a day to move quickly enough.

I've worked jobs where I've watched the clock and it is painstaking. Currently, I cannot do all that I want to accomplish in a day and this is every day of my life. I wish that I had about twenty hours each day to just "work." They do not teach this way of thinking in most colleges. My concept of the 15-year sprint will show you how. Now, if you have the awareness and drive early enough, you can start in your early 20s. But the truth is you can start at any time in your life. Fifteen years go by faster than we think, and we have more opportunities than we think.

If you're curious about starting in your 20s, here's what that could look like. From age 15 to 25, stay curious about yourself and what you like to do, and have an open mind. Look at this world and see what gets you excited. That is the field where you need to work. Some fields afford the opportunity to find a problem or problems that you can solve for people. Others may just give you the opportunity to enjoy what you do. Change your educational direction or even change your major in college if you figure out your soul purpose or at the least your passion while you're still in college.

I hear and see so many people quit or give up due to age. Realize that there are people who did not start working at a job that they were passionate about until after they retired from a job that they had worked at all of their life but were not passionate about.

You can change directions and never should feel locked into a job. Additionally, it may take you longer than age 25 to figure out your passion and that's ok. And most importantly, do not put age restrictions on yourself. Do not paint yourself into a specific age for retirement. I share my targets and numbers here for your guidance and to show you what is possible.

My counsel is to spend your teens and early 20s exploring areas of interest, trying different things, moving toward your soul purpose, and making a bigger picture plan. That will enable you to go hard for fifteen years, from about 25 to about 40, executing your plan. From there you can be set to retire (or not) and do whatever you want in life.

I plan to start new businesses and form many new entities after 75 or 80 years of age. I am not handcuffing myself with "I will be too old to start over or start something new at age 60 or 65." Retirement is not defined properly and should not be thought of as an age. Mom and I retired in our early 40s. I would even argue that I retired at age 28. When would you like to retire?

If at all possible, and if you can be comfortable with the responsibility, I recommend working for yourself. You can make (and keep) more money working for yourself, but more importantly, you can make your own hours and be your own boss. I want you to work at a couple of jobs to know what it is like to work for someone. You will then, most likely, want to work for yourself.

And remember, you can start from anywhere. I started from $300 thousand in debt and am on my way to achieving unimaginable wealth.

## 📍 CHALLENGE TO YOU

SEEK OUT AND TALK WITH successful people 65 and older. Ask them about their best and worst life choices—what they would do again, what they would change, and what they would skip. Ask the same questions and look for similar and different answers. Look for grandparents, friends' grandparents, at weddings, grocery stores, wherever. Start the dialogue, and do your own research on how you want to live after 65. Aim for eight people.

Next, do a quick analysis of the last 15 years of your life. Where were you 15 years ago, and where are you now? What skills have you substantially up-leveled in that time? What interests have shifted and which ones have stayed the same? What do you like to do? What subjects or hobbies do you enjoy? How do you like to spend your time? This exercise will give you a sense of both how fast and how slow 15 years go by; how much can change and what also can stay constant. It will give you a sense of what is possible for the next 15.

Also, if you are reading this after you are out and on your own, write your first budget. Include your income and your expenses: school, housing, food—both groceries and dining out, entertainment, phone, wifi, electricity, car, rental, and health insurance, subscriptions, car, gas, public transportation, and clothes. One way to do this is to review your credit and debit card statements for 12 months prior—this will give you an idea of your monthly spending, and your annual spending. You may be surprised at how your favorite $15 salad from someplace, with a drink, tax, and tip, adds up to a $240 monthly expense for example. For now, we are not looking to make changes, but rather to gather the information. I do not want you to live on a budget, but you need to understand the flow of money for yourself before trying to understand revenue, expenses, profits, and losses of businesses.

# THE CONVENTIONAL TIMELINE IS ALL WRONG

MOST PEOPLE GET SOME OR all of the timeline for life *wrong*. And no one talks about it til it's way too late. How is it that my Mamaw and Papaw were so productive their whole lives and barely made ends meet, ever? And so active their entire lives, and then just—not?

Watching their rapid decline in a stark, prison-like retirement home had a profound, life-changing effect on me. I began deeply questioning the ways of the world—the conventions, the path expected of me, and my future, including life after 65. It was unusual to be thinking about that as much as I did as a teenager, but I'm glad I did. I take the approach not very different from filmmakers and plan not only the end but the whole show, from the beginning. I want maximum enjoyment and entertainment, and I bet you do, too.

Retirement is an empty promise that we'll have this financial freedom and can live and enjoy life at age 65, after working our butts off for 40+ years, and with the help of retirement investments and social security. I just don't buy it.

## THE 15-YEAR SPRINT

INSTEAD OF FOLLOWING CONVENTION, I set a goal at age 26 to step on the gas and build my wealth for the next 15 years, so that I could then do whatever I wanted for the rest of my life. Fifteen years is 780 weeks, which may seem inconceivable now. Just think of your last 15 years—depending on when you're reading this book, it could be around the time you started kindergarten.

Think about how much is possible if you have the structure in place and the drive to achieve something: education, sports, a social life, faith, the start of a business or career. There's so much growth, learning and fun to be had, and that doesn't have to fall off a cliff or shackle you to debt as our societal norms may have you believe.

The goal is to take the focus off instant rewards and pay attention to planning, productivity, and playing the long game. I wanted to achieve wealth before I was too old to enjoy it. And to do so, I had some big changes to make. The first was my mindset.

## COMPARE & CONTRAST

### The 65+ Retirement Nirvana Fantasy

Many people believe that you party hard and have the most fun you can in high school and college, then raise kids and work hard all your adult life with minimal or moderate fun, then retire and enjoy life again after 65. This ideation of retirement doesn't make sense—not if you want to have fun your whole life.

Let's break down the issues with this line of thinking:

Partying and fun in high school and college—this could lead to alcohol, drugs, sex (because you are not thinking straight while drunk), loss of needed sleep for healthy thinking in school, and so on.

At best, having too much of this kind of "fun" can keep you from being able to reach your full potential in the main adult part of your life. What I mean is that if you make bad grades or fail a subject, then you will have to redo those subjects and postpone the next steps of your life. At worst, you could end up in prison, an addict, an alcoholic, or have a child which can drastically affect the rest of your life.

Raising kids and working hard your adult life—most dedicate around 40 to 50 years to working and living from paycheck to paycheck and 20 to 25 years of this time they are also raising children.

There is nothing wrong with working to make money and you will enjoy being with and raising your children, but the way most people take on this part of their life is not a fun way. They justify this part of life by planning to enjoy the retirement years of life.

Retiring to enjoy life—this is great in theory, but a Motley Fool Article published in August of 2022 "Average Retirement Savings in the U.S.: $65,000" stated that in 2019 the average retirement savings was at $65,000. I personally believe that 90%

or more Americans retire with inadequate savings and many will retire with little to no savings. These people are stuck with any social security and whatever they possibly scrounged up toward the end of their working career to be relegated to a fixed income in their retirement years.

Retirement becomes a time in which one does not have to work, but little money is available for the enjoyment part of retirement. With no preparation and planning, you will have this type of life because it is the default that our society has in place and if you don't actively choose something else, this is where you'll arrive.

### Step on the Gas for a 15-year Sprint

The proper way to go through the progression of life, in my opinion, is to enjoy every phase as much as possible without hurting the next phases. A good plan would be:

1) Enjoy high school and college while being conscious of your big-picture goals and working toward the adult phase of life. So, go out and have as much fun as you possibly can while making sure you get enough sleep and study time to do well in school. Staying away from drugs, sex, and alcohol can't hurt. Remember, this is a Dad talking here. At a minimum, make conscious and cautious choices. If you look at any successful entrepreneur, you will see that they kept the things that would hurt their spiritual and educational growth to a minimum, or most did not indulge at all.

2) The adult stage of life where you raise kids and work to make a living, can be the most enjoyable and fun time of your life. Owning your own business frees up time to see your kids' school plays, watch all their sports events and games, as well as being able to travel whenever you like. You will be able to afford babysitters to go out on weekly dates with your spouse. This is the age of life where you should enjoy yourself and not be bogged down with having to struggle to put food on the table.

3) Planning and investing will give the retirement portion of your life a totally different outlook. You can have what everyone longs for in retirement, but only if you have done everything correctly in the first two phases of life. You want to be able to be free of any work and have the money to do what you want. I will go a step further and tell you that wealthy people do not retire in a traditional sense. Instead, they find financial independence at a younger age and are then free to enjoy the rest of their life.

I would suggest that you sit down at least annually (in January of each year) and adjust old goals and do new goals for 1, 5, 10, and 20 years out. I also suggest doing a personal financial statement at the same time. You can start with income and spending. This will build awareness of a 12-month view of finances and is critical for you to understand not just buying your next meal or outfit, but the bigger financial picture for yourself. As I have gotten older, I have found myself updating my goals and personal financial statement more frequently, which is now done quarterly.

I want you to learn as a teenager the importance of producing, investing, and most of all, the art of planning for your future/retirement. I don't think about retirement as most of society does, and certainly not in a conventional way, and I don't want you to, either. I feel like I am in retirement already.

Retirement to me is the point in which you are financially independent, meaning that you have enough investment income/profit to cover your living expenses and not drain any of the principles of the investments without having to physically work for any money. So, instead of saving for retirement at 65 or 70, I want you to invest for your future, which could mean retiring earlier than I did at age 41.

If nothing else, think of this example of a Friday night babysitting job. Let's say it's four hours. As a parent, you'd be doing that "babysitting job", at a 6X multiple (24 hours) per day, times seven days per week, times 52 weeks per year. That's if you don't plan and haven't built in extra income to afford a babysitter. That means no time for yourself or your spouse. In that mode, parenting, which should be a great joy, is exhausting and all-consuming. In contrast, with a little forward-thinking and planning, you can have all that you want.

## THE ILLUSION

ONE FIRST MUST UNDERSTAND THAT most people live a life of illusion. They have allowed others to form who they are at the core of their being. They have been a follower of conventions for all of their lives to the point where they have become the puppets that society has taught them to be. They live a false life and do not even realize that this life has forced them to be a consumer who lives a life of scarcity.

Let me explain. Most people have been fed a picture of their ideal life. It's been programmed into them. Much of it comes from our government-driven conventions and the media.

Most think that life is about making good money. Most also become really great consumers, yet live a life of scarcity. This means they buy all the things that are perceived as necessities—the nicest car, the best house, the brand-name clothes, appliances, and accessories. But many buy these things just a little beyond their means, every time. Think of adding up a 10% more expensive house, 15% more expensive furniture, and 20% higher price on a car—it all adds up and leads to chronic debt. Parents think this and teach this because that is what society and their parents taught them: school, good grades, university, 9 to 5, commute, consume.

Big pharma. Big debt. Small retirement.

The fantasy is that this will bring you happiness, peace, and all the possessions you want. That is how it's programmed. That's how it's marketed. That's what it looks like in the news, movies, and media. But it's just not how it translates in reality. Not in the hours of your day, the dollars in your bank account, or the quality of your years.

We need a new recipe. A new timeline. And to do that, you must start by practicing awareness and increasing your conscious choices on a regular basis.

## THE SEDUCTION OF MARKETING

PART OF LIVING IN A capitalist society means everything we do or are involved in has been motivated in some way to market and sell products to make the almighty dollar. Our world is built on marketing and selling products. Consider, outside of spirituality and doing for others, that everything we do is done to either make money for ourselves or to help someone else make money. If you can understand this and put it into perspective, then life can be much easier and much less stressful for you.

**Convenience**

Convenience is a modern convention. Many things we do now are driven by what companies have invented or developed to make something easy for us to do. The one-click buys, next-day delivery, unlimited, on-demand streaming, pre-made meals, auto-ship, and the list goes on.

**Shoes**

We want a certain brand of shoes that someone we consider a celebrity or someone that we admire wears. We buy that brand instead of buying a shoe that fits well, feels good, and can be purchased at a great price. A pair of shoes costs around $20 to $30 to make no matter what brand is attached to them. Sure, there may be a few exceptions for shoes that require more technical work or some expensive material, but in general, shoes are not expensive to make. However, we will pay $100, $200, $500, or more than $2,000 for a single pair of shoes due to branding. Companies spend fortunes paying celebrities and athletes to wear a brand of shoes just to get us to want them.

**News**

We pay to watch the news. While watching the news, companies are paying tons of money to advertise to us to use their service or buy their products. On the actual news program, someone is interviewed. That person being interviewed is either being paid to be on the news program or has some interest in being on the program to help themselves or the company they work for to make money. The news headlines are benefitting the news station in some way. They are providing the news to make money. We need to understand that all we are bombarded with daily, hourly, and even by the minute prompts us to do something that will help someone else make money.

**Medicine**

There is nothing that is void of marketing at this point. Look what has become of medicine. It is hard to watch TV without being bombarded with pharmaceuticals and health insurance commercials in every block of commercials. When did it become a good idea for a patient to go to the doctor's office and request prescription drugs based on TV commercials? Are people not hearing the side effects? Should that be the way of medicine?

Look at dentistry and dental hygiene as another example of marketing controlling our decisions and how our society functions. Insurance companies ran studies years ago to determine how often a patient needed a dental exam. They did not want to pay for exams but determined that paying for regular exams saved money that they would have to pay out for bigger dental procedures that went unnoticed without regular exams. So, they came up with an average of six months between dental exams to pay the minimal amount of money out for their clients (the patients). Therefore, neither we as patients nor the dentists decide on the proper timeframe for us to visit a dentist or get a dental exam, instead, the insurance companies dictate and we allow it.

**Influencers**

Anything we watch on TV or see on social media is a form of marketing. When an actor is interviewed on a morning news show or late-night TV show, they are not there out of the goodness of their heart. They are there to promote a new movie or TV show.

**Industrial Complexes**

In addition, there are big brands, big pharma, the educational industrial complex, the food industrial complex, the alcohol industrial complex, and more. It's dizzying.

**Church**

Even within churches, it's important to understand that they all are businesses. Churches would not be viable if they did not have money, which is collected as tithe. I believe many non-Christians or even Christians that do not attend church, have the feelings or thoughts that why tithe and pay the preacher to buy a house, a car, food, etc. Some pastors do take advantage of tithes, but I would hope that this is not the case for most.

My personal opinion is that churches are businesses and have to do projections, market, have a budget, and do everything that is the definition of a business. The difference between a business and a proper church is that the church is a non-profit that functions from tax-deductible donations (tithes). Most importantly, the church functions within a budget as strictly as possible to stay viable and all other money received is used to "market" Christ to the world in many different ways.

## TEENS BEWARE

ESPECIALLY FOR TEENS, IT IS easy to fall into the trap of we should do something, own something, or be part of something because it is the norm, it's what everyone else is doing, it's what makes us cool, etc. This only grows with us and gets worse as we get older, unless we become aware and make a conscious decision to not allow ourselves to be controlled by outside marketing to form our lives and how we live daily.

## MAKING CONSCIOUS CHOICES

MARKETING AND CONVENIENCE ARE MODERN conventions that steal conscious choice if we're not careful. The reason I'm pointing this out is because I want you to think about it, consider it, and make a conscious decision to have opinions and make purchasing decisions without being influenced. This is almost impossible unless you get in a habit of seeing through the marketing ploy and then do and buy what you want to buy or do without the marketing influence.

The beginning of mankind's life started as easy and simple. However, we've pushed to complicate life as much as possible throughout time. We have more stressors in our lives now than ever before in history. Phones have brought ease and comfort to our lives, but they have also made it easier for us to worry, be more envious seeing what others are doing, take away from personal time with family and friends, add stress with more to do in less time, and on and on.

It boils down to the fact that we need to take control of what we want and need. We need to think and do for ourselves and not just blindly walk through this world without knowing what we want to get out of our lives. Our society has gotten so lazy and ignorant about what we truly want and need. Our society wants to consume and do as little as possible to get what we want. Sitting on a phone or in front of a TV, eating, and sleeping has become our underlying goal in life. The thought has become "I will work just enough to get what I want out of life." "I will produce as little as possible while consuming as much as possible."

This is where learning how to be a producer and have an abundance mindset, explained in chapters 6 and 7, will lead you to more conscious choices in your life.

I cannot stress enough how much I want you to make conscious choices. You cannot do this while allowing the world around you to win by marketing to you. There are many great things in life that have helped me to be free, happy, and satisfied, but the one important thing that I can contribute to my freedom, contentment, and happiness is not allowing the outside world to control my thoughts, wants, and needs through marketing. A high-end car, a pair of shoes, who you are seen with, and where you are seen will never give you satisfaction. Instead, it will create an empty need for more. When you can be happy being you and buying and doing what you want to do, instead of what you think others want you to do or want from you, you will then have this unburdened freedom that is so satisfying. I feel that we must understand that earthly possessions are borrowed for a period of time and they are not what is important in life.

If you are able to find freedom with this understanding, your mindset changes and you become wealthy. Wealthy in life, wealthy in how you live life. Wealth is not becoming rich monetarily, but a state of mind. If this is accomplished, stress is then snuffed out. It becomes easier to obtain financial wealth when wealth is a mindset!

We must notice and understand these outside influences, make a conscious decision to not allow them to influence us, and realize that if we do not make goals and plans for ourselves to become who we want to be then we lose control of our lives and our futures.

Otherwise, we must realize that the default will be that we become followers and that we allow outside influences to form us. We are then like remote-controlled zombies that are just going through life with no focus and no reason to live. Dramatic? Yes. Accurate? Yes.

##  CHALLENGE TO YOU

MY CHALLENGE TO YOU IS to continue reading this book and absorb these ideas and concepts. Consider how you can bridge the gap between where you are and where you want to be, and what it would look like for you to retire by age 40, then really have fun and get really wealthy doing what you love that makes you a lot of money in the process.

# 3

# MY RECIPE

The ingredients for chocolate mousse are cream, chocolate, eggs, sugar, and salt. Very simple. If you combine these things in the right proportion at the right temperature, you will get a creamy, delicious dessert.

But do you know that if you use room-temperature cream, it will turn out soupy and speckled? The cream has to be cold, and it's best mixed in a chilled glass bowl before you add the other ingredients. That's how you get the thick, airy, pastry-chef-level chocolate mousse.

The concepts shared in the following chapters are the cream, eggs, sugar, chocolate, and salt of wealth. That's to say, they are mainstay components that surprise no one, but like a great pastry chef, it's how you prepare and combine these ingredients that makes all the difference in a successful outcome.

Like in wealth building, it's not just the "what" but also the how, when, and at what temperature you do things. No one wants to eat a bag of salt by itself. Sugar, either, despite its addictive qualities. Consider Italian, French, and Belgian pâtisseries, where only the pastry chef who has completed a lengthy training process, typically an apprenticeship, and passed a written examination can call themselves a *pâtissier*, a master pastry chef.

## ANYONE CAN BECOME WEALTHY

WEALTH, HOWEVER, IS DIFFERENT. ANYONE can become wealthy. Case in point: me. How is it that someone with an undiagnosed learning disability, the last to read in his class, and $300,000 in debt in his early 20s is now well on the path to $300,000,000 in wealth?

That's right, Mom and I started out with $150,000 in student debt between my undergrad and her dental school. Then, we got a home loan for another $150,000 to build a house. Fortunately, her parents were willing to take a chance on us and sign as guarantors. And there we were—early 20s and $300,000 in debt.

In a 15-year timespan, we've transformed our entire financial picture by making very specific choices and taking very specific actions toward building our financial wealth. We've been very successful and are on a path to $300,000,000 of net worth with an ultimate goal of over $1,000,000,000 of net worth. Thus, our belief is that a 15-year sprint can work for virtually anyone willing to work for it. We have had some big successes, but also some gut-punch lessons to get where we are now. The 15-year timeframe gave us ample room to recover from failures and get back to thriving. But the biggest failure, in my opinion, would've been taking a conventional path.

Had we followed convention, we would've both worked full-time jobs for the last 25 years and have 20 more years of grueling work ahead of us. Meanwhile, we'd have scrimped and saved to pay off that debt, maybe incur new debt to buy a cabin "up north" somewhere, and if we were "lucky"—we would be retiring with a moderate cushion. That's the norm. That's the convention.

But guess what—Mom and I weren't down for convention.

At 25, when the joke was I hadn't picked up more than one book, I started picking up a few more books. I also started attending several seminars and growing my knowledge.

At that time, I had wanted to pursue a music career. When I saw I wasn't going to be the next Jon Bon Jovi, I was still committed to my obsession with living a good life after 65—not to mention, having a blast along the way. After reaching $300 million in financial wealth the next goal is over $1 billion. I didn't see how making that kind of leap in my bank account could involve conventional thinking in career and finance. Very few things on that path did. This is why I wrote this book and spelled out this special recipe for you.

In contrast to having worked 40+ hour weeks for the last many years and scraping by, we paid off our debt years ago, own several homes, were both present raising you, have several passive income streams, and are still growing by leaps and bounds. Some may call this work. Some may call it hard work. I call it making conscious decisions and living my best life.

## TIME

THE ONE FINITE THING THAT we cannot overcome is time. I can show you how to make a trillion dollars, but I might not be able to show you how to do it in your lifetime, without outside help and luck. It takes time to build businesses, time to nurture relationships, and time to grow one's educational, spiritual, mental, and physical states. The earlier you consider this in life—the easier you can make it on yourself. Sort of like refrigerating the heavy cream and a glass bowl the night before you go to make a masterpiece chocolate mousse.

Other factors that we might not overcome are physical challenges or mental hurdles. If we can work around those three hurdles, time, physical, and mental challenges, then we can accomplish anything we put our minds to if we follow the recipe.

Mom and I have spent our lives discussing our thoughts and growth together. I hope to not only give you a better understanding of Mom's and my thoughts and vision but to also help you to think about your growth and where you want to be when you are our age.

I also hope that you will have a better understanding of the importance of joy and love, how they are based on spirituality, and how it is the foundation and first priority of attaining success and great wealth in all aspects of your life. I hope this book will truly be a roadmap for you to not only attain great wealth in all aspects of life but to show how simple it is to have success with the right recipe.

In our case, we are always looking one, five, ten, and twenty years out. That's the only way to get ahead of the ticking clock and make it easier on yourself.

## SCRAMBLED EGGS VS A CAKE

EGGS ARE GREAT FOR BREAKFAST, my preference is scrambled. While I enjoy eggs, using eggs as an ingredient with other ingredients can produce something even greater. You can use cream, eggs, sugar, chocolate, and salt to make chocolate mousse or a cake. The same concept applies to the ingredients of wealth.

Considering only one ingredient or recipe or following one path may get you stuck in a rut. The great thing about learning how to self-direct your education, either inside or outside of traditional schools, is that you can consider a variety of different thought processes—even opposites. You can learn from master chefs as diverse as Bobby Flay and Masaharu Morimoto. When you do that, you can take what you like from each and ultimately make your own recipes.

That's exactly what I did by following a "master chef" in the wealth world by using the four key wealth "ingredients," listed below. I'll share the overarching themes from each, and show you how I combine them, then break tasks down to the smallest parts in a monthly, weekly, daily, and even hourly schedule.

The main ingredients to wealth, as I see them and discuss in this book, are:

1) The Five Wealths
2) SMART Goals
3) Abundance vs. Scarcity Mindset
4) Productive and Consumptive Time Use

Putting all of these together is what makes it work. Taking what has been noted, the five wealths, abundance, productivity, and then adding goals and plans with scheduling and tasks is "the special sauce" for me. There are very successful people who do not need to write down their goals or daily tasks, but those people either are great at mentally keeping goals and tasks or have an assistant who does that for them.

Each of these concepts (including goals and plans) is beneficial on its own—but together they are all supercharged. Using all of these concepts together is what allows me to hit my peak performance.

You can set any goal in life and if there is enough time, you will be able to obtain the goal. We will take complex and unmanageable examples and break them down into simple processes and procedures to get them accomplished.

## KEY DISTINCTION: "A WEALTH MASTER CHEF" FOR ME

I WAS USING SOME PORTION of these concepts in my life since my 20s. However, I was completely unaware of the framework, that I was doing them, or how to repeat it to amp up my results. My elaborate marriage proposal to your Mom, which I talk about in Chapter 5, is an example of that. I didn't call it a SMART goal, it's just what I was doing.

In my mid-20s, as I started picking up books, I became more aware that there were frameworks and mindsets that would amplify my efforts to make money and find success in life. Many books talk about SMART goals. Many others talk about an abundance mindset. These concepts are as old as dirt, and they are mainstays for a reason.

When I first saw concepts or heard of ideas that could help me, I could not fully understand the importance and the real impact that putting those ideas and concepts to work could really provide for me. However, when I attended multi-millionaire entrepreneur Garrett Gunderson's Conference in Salt Lake City in 2010 when I was 36 years old, everything changed for me. I came to understand how these concepts, used together, were the way to supercharge all of my efforts. And in the last 12 years, I've found that to be absolutely true. I've put my own spin on it to make it work for me, and now I want you to make it work for you, starting much earlier than I did.

## TWO SCHOOLS OF THOUGHT

I'VE CONSISTENTLY LOOKED TO TWO experts in financial help on my journey: Garrett, as mentioned, whose focus is on wealth building, and Dave Ramsey, who is known for helping people reduce and eliminate debt. I've used both of their philosophies at different stages of my growth, supplemented by numerous other self-directed readings on the subject.

The perspectives of these two are different, almost to the point of being extreme opposites when it comes to becoming debt-free. Garrett teaches the ways to become financially wealthy using productive investments—that is: spending money to make money and producing more, while Dave preaches and teaches budgeting and working to cut debts to become debt-free.

Both want to help individuals achieve financial freedom or financial independence—albeit with totally different approaches. I believe they each are perfect for certain situations within different demographics, it is important to understand that either/or is much better than having no recipe whatsoever and the alternative of not working toward financial freedom or financial independence. I have been a big proponent and follower of each line of thinking at different times in my life. Both are perfect for the right people at the proper stage in their lives.

The concepts, like the others presented in this book, are as old as dirt, and they work for a reason: they are a strong foundation. But like chocolate and cream, it's not just the "what," it's the "how" to use them and to use them to create your own successful recipe. Your focus over the years will shift, but if you follow these fundamentals and the "how" and "when" of using them, you can't go wrong.

**Dave's Way**

Dave focuses on the majority of demographics in our society—those who are in debt. They have debt on credit cards, cars, homes, tuition, etc. Dave's goal is to help the majority of our society become debt-free through scrimping and saving. Dave preaches that we should get out of debt and never go into debt for any reason. He also teaches to take on a second or third job if necessary to attack debt. Dave is 100% against any debt in any form.

The basics are that we need to crawl before walking and Dave teaches how to become financially responsible through setting a budget and working off any consumer debt. He stresses the importance of having six months of expenses in savings to cover unexpected expenses or loss of income. He then takes on paying off all consumer debt and then house mortgage to be completely debt-free. Again, this is great for most of our society that is out of control with debt.

Getting a bit deeper with these teachings, Dave's work focuses on people who are consumers who are in debt, again a high percentage of our society. For this group of people, it is a perfect teaching and very important for those people to strive to get out of debt. These are people who would not be able to get out of debt and change the way they live without a major shift in thinking and teachings such as Dave's.

**Garrett's Way**

Garrett, on the other hand, is focused on a much smaller demographic who have already conquered the debt issue. Garrett's goal is to help 1,000,000 people become financially independent through production and increasing revenue without necessarily sacrificing costs to do so. Garrett teaches that one can grow revenue and not be so concerned with cutting expenses.

Cutting back is more of a scarcity mindset and not an abundance mindset. Garrett does not specify that it is important to budget, but instead, one should plan and goal to increase one's income. Garrett believes that growing profits is not dependent on budgeting and cutting expenses.

Garrett does not dissuade his clients or readers from borrowing money if it is used to grow. I am not saying he is a proponent of productive debt. Additionally, Garrett is teaching a more global mindset shift to abundance over scarcity and growing wealth in all aspects of our lives, not just financially.

There is a small number of people (1% or maybe a little more) who do not have an issue with debt. These people understand productive debt and can thrive on productive debt without getting into any type of consumer debt. Productive debt is one of the only ways to grow some businesses properly or at all.

## MY TAKE

IN THE BEGINNING, OUT OF school and saddled with $300k in debt, I followed Dave Ramsey and reached a point of being debt-free of everything but a house mortgage, but transitioned quickly into staying consumer debt-free but leveraging great amounts of debt to grow productively.

I currently owe nothing on automobiles and other consumer debt, but I do have debt on our residential real estate along with many other commercial real estate properties and other businesses.

There is a way to incorporate 90 percent of both Dave Ramsey and Garrett Gunderson's teachings.

We worked in Dave's realm of thinking from college graduation until we were around 29 to 30 years old. That is when we opened our first business and took on business debt. I have a mindset of not having any debt that does not make me money. So, business debt, in general, does make money and is what I consider productive debt. Of course, there are bad business deals that lose money and I have made my fair share of those. It is never fun closing a business where you still owe $500,000, $1,000,000, $10,000,000, or even $100,000,000.

I began setting goals and planning with our first business and this allowed us to purchase or start at least one business every year since. What I began doing with goals and plans in business and with our personal finances was very similar to what Garrett teaches in Wealth Factory. Garrett really helped me view wealth in a more global aspect to expand the same processes from financial to all five wealths, which I'll share more about in Chapter 4.

## IT'S LIKE AN EXAM… SORT OF

THINK OF THE MISSION OF making a good grade on an exam. Exams at all levels of school were harder and more stressful for me than starting a new business is now. All of the information that I was going to be tested on in a week was extremely daunting and an almost impossible feeling to achieve.

Most of this, if not all, was me not understanding and following a recipe or formula for success in approaching an exam. I did not plan. I did not break my learning into small bite-sized pieces. I did not have a timeline.

Instead, I procrastinated and tried to cram it into a time period that was too short. This led to stress, anxiety, and worry, all of which took away from the small amount of time I had to study.

I never figured out that studying and finding ways to get information into my memory bank daily, starting from the first day of the semester, would have made an exam so much easier. This was tough enough in high school, but adding independence, less sleep, parties, and all the other activities of college, and I wonder how I made it.

Frankly, it is amazing that anyone makes it. All of this underscores the importance of breaking tasks down into bite-sized pieces and having a recipe or formula that makes the seemingly impossible actually possible.

## WHY PEOPLE FAIL AT FINANCIAL SUCCESS

AS A SOCIETY, OUR MINDSET is broken. At a young age, we are taught—programmed—that consuming goods and services—being a consumer—will bring happiness. Our world revolves around how businesses and individuals can sell things to us. Convenience has become a new currency.

There is nothing wrong with marketing and selling goods and services. This is capitalism at work. But how it's done, and how it's been normalized in our culture, particularly in the U.S., is at unprecedented levels compared to the rest of the world.

Simply put, we're addicted to consuming. Food, alcohol, games, household goods, clothes, shoes, cars, sports equipment, TV, movies, you name it. So addicted that we use credit and go into debt we can't afford, which is consumerism at the max. The problem is that consumerism kills any chance to reach financial success.

Financial success is becoming financially free or independent. When one reaches a point where they have enough money to cover their standard of living without actively working for this money, that is financial independence.

## CHALLENGE TO YOU

THINK ABOUT HOW THE RECIPE concept applies to what you are already doing. As you go through the following chapters, take note of the ways you are already doing these concepts— you are likely doing many of these things, and may not be aware of this framework. Or, you may be doing some of these things. However few or many you are doing, we want to celebrate what's going right, and then use that to build from.

Anchor in your reference points. Think and imagine what it could look like to do them consciously and fully. What could be possible for you? And then do them all together. There's nothing immediate to change or do, the challenge is to build your awareness of what's already working for you, and then think about what is possible if you apply these to your own 15-year wealth sprint.

# PART 2

## Learn the Key Lessons of Wealth Building

# 4

# THE 5 WEALTHS

THE WORD "WEALTH" MOST OFTEN brings to mind an image of money and things: cash, robust bank accounts, houses, cars, furniture, and clothes. It certainly did for me as a teen. Success to me at that time was in the aspect of money only. I wanted to have enough money to have things that successful people had, like a big house, nice cars, a boat, and eventually a private plane bigger than anyone else's in my small town.

This cannot be stated enough! True wealth is about a lot more than money. In tough financial times, when you have little income and especially when you have debt, it can feel like money is the only type of wealth that matters. I assure you, it's not.

This concept was ingrained in me long before I ever heard of the five wealths, and I learned it one night in junior high.

See, growing up, my dad was overprotective. He would get upset easily for very little to no reason. He was overly suspicious about people talking behind his back. Since he worked for the phone company, he tapped our home phone line and recorded every conversation we had without our knowing. We would wonder how he knew things that were said privately or confidentially to friends or family and later found out about the phone tap. He was also verbally and physically abusive.

One night, I tried to step in between him, my mom, and a plastic baseball bat, as she tried to hunker down between the wall and the toilet. It was a school night. I was around 10 years old. He kicked us out of the house. We ran out with nothing in hand in order to escape any more bats, belts, or fists.

Mom had a baby carrier and my sister in hand along with me and my brother. I remember her putting on makeup in our minivan to cover the black eye so she could go into the Holiday Inn and reserve a room for us to sleep that night. The next morning, we had to time it just right to go back home late enough that he had left for work, and early enough to change before going to school.

This was early enough into the abuse that my mom was too embarrassed to tell anyone what was going on. Within a year or two, she finally broke down and we went to my Granddaddy's (my mom's dad's) when we had to flee the house. It was incidents like these that led to the darkest time in my life.

One night in junior high, I was so mad and upset that all I wanted to do was show my dad he could not control or hurt me anymore. I lay in bed and held a loaded 22 revolver to my temple with my finger on the trigger. I cried for an hour or so, wanting to pull the trigger to stop the pain.

I finally realized that I could not pull the trigger for much better reasons that had nothing to do with my dad. I never got close to any feelings of suicide after that one time, but it is scary to believe how close I was that night.

If I had drank a couple of beers, done any type of drugs, or had no belief in God, I would not have been able to clearly understand or think through the reasons not to pull the trigger. I did not drink beer or any alcohol until late my junior year in high school and never tried drugs. I grew up regularly attending church and became a Christian at age 10 during vacation bible school. My mom, brother, and sister, as well as my faith, kept me from being a statistic that night.

It may seem strange to relay this story in the context of the five wealths, but it demonstrates my take on it: wealth is not about money.

Without relationships, spirituality, and health, you only have a fractional picture of wealth. Relationships, spirituality, health, and education are all part of the greater wealth picture, plus money. Money may bring some peace, joy, and happiness, but ultimate peace, joy, and happiness in the long term do not come just from money.

There are other ways to break these down but these five wealths are what I base my life on, in order of priority.

#1—Spiritual Wealth
#2—Relationship Wealth
#3—Health Wealth
#4—Educational Wealth
#5—Financial Wealth

## THE SECRET SAUCE

FOR ME, WHEN I ALIGN all five wealths and work on them together, I see results quicker. Earlier on, I had worked to achieve one or two wealths separately, but working toward all of them together along with SMART goals (detailed in the next chapter) is where I really began seeing exponential growth in all aspects of wealth.

It's always important for me to set high goals while realizing small "bite-sized" wins on the way to the goals. I feel that when we recognize these small wins, it gives us more fuel for our drive and persistence.

The five wealths have been around forever individually and in different forms. Different people have referenced and taught different aspects, but Garrett Gunderson is who introduced me to the five wealths as a global understanding of true wealth, and that it's based on relationships with family, and then with friends. The broader reach for wealth includes mental and physical wealth. After the first four wealths are attained, then financial wealth can be attained.

I recommend prioritizing these five wealths in the order listed above. Any individual can have wealth or be successful in any or maybe two or three of these, but I feel that true wealth can only be reached by being successful in all five of these aspects.

Striving to achieve all five wealths together is really never achieved and done. Rather, it's a continuous work in progress—we achieve higher levels of wealth as we grow. If I were to ask you what does it mean to be rich, your answer would be different than most others. There is no specific amount to being rich. If

I ask you how or when you first tried to be rich, what would your answer be?

My point is that all five aspects of wealth, like being rich, are not something really accomplished, but something we are always working toward. I guess there are those who would have a definitive answer for achieving some parts of the wealths, just as some would have a specific number of what rich represents.

But in my mind, being wealthy or being rich will never really be fully achieved. I can say that I am more wealthy than most because I have achieved high levels of all five wealths. However, as soon as I reach a goal or a level, I set new goals or new levels for myself in wealth.

Using the recipe concept, you can attain these wealths through goals, plans, projections, mini-goals, and budgeting or reverse budgeting.

## SPIRITUAL WEALTH

SPIRITUAL WEALTH IS THE FIRST priority for me. Faith is number one in my life and I hope it is in yours.

If you are spiritually wealthy you know and give love and joy. You have a firm foundation of morals and integrity. You realize that we are here for a short time and the earthly possessions are gifts. And that the gifts should not be accumulated and idolized, but used as a good steward for ultimate good. Everything else in life is built on this foundation.

Being spiritually wealthy will give you love and joy, as well as freedom. I am able to live life in abundance and I am certain it comes from my foundation in spirituality. In order to be spiritually wealthy, we need to understand the need to love God first, love ourselves second, and then we are able to give and show love to all others.

My personal belief is that everything is based on God and Christianity. This being the case, I have made it my business for spirituality to be the number one priority. Others who read this book may have other spiritual beliefs. Great. Having a close relationship with God or a higher power can only happen when we purposefully make it our priority.

## RELATIONSHIP WEALTH

Relationship wealth is the second priority in my view. Having a relationship with God is the spiritual wealth, but having relationships with others is important as well. Wealth is having a wonderful and loving relationship with your immediate family and extended family and then friends.

There are also some situations where stepping away from a relationship instead of into a relationship is what is best for your personal well-being. This does not mean that we do not love and show love to these people in our lives, but we just step away from them slowly and nicely, if it is better for our wealth journey and specifically the joy that we have in our lives.

## PHYSICAL OR HEALTH WEALTH

Physical or health wealth is next on my list of prioritized wealths. Being fit and healthy is very important to our well-being and our joy but more importantly, it helps to keep you young and energetic. It is hard to work on the other wealths if you are struggling with your health. I look at my health with gratification that I have the health that I possess. One has to feel comfortable in their own skin in order to obtain joy at times.

Health wealth has two major components. What we put in our bodies and how we use our bodies. It is easy to not concern ourselves with either what we eat and drink or how we treat our bodies. So, it is important to make a conscious effort to work for both.

A quick Google search of a connection between physical health and financial wealth provides many articles with research connecting the two. I have many thoughts and ideas on this connection but will not get into the weeds here. The bottom line, physical health wealth is very important to joy, longevity, and financial wealth.

## EDUCATIONAL WEALTH

EDUCATION IS ANOTHER TOPIC NOT frequently considered in relation to financial freedom and stress levels. However, I cannot overstate this next statement. If I had to point out the one thing that has helped me to achieve an amazing and unbelievable amount of ultimate wealth, it would be education. Not high school or college, but reading or more specifically listening to audiobooks on topics that help me with each of the wealths. I can without a doubt say that I would not be wealthy, without working on my education after college. It's the way to true education wealth.

This will help you to excel and be successful throughout life. The right books and courses will help you to move toward productivity and away from consumerism. It will definitely help the overall health of your wealths.

Education in perspective is just realizing that it needs to be part of your life of growth. I read or listen to the Bible for at least 15 minutes a day or one hour to an hour and a half each week. I listen to non-fiction books 30 minutes a day or two to two and a half hours a week. I also do educational apps that include growing my vocabulary, learning Spanish, sharpening my mind, and more for at least 15 minutes per day. I also play the guitar 30 minutes a day and try to write music an hour to four hours a month. I write this book and other books daily for at least an hour.

I used to brag that I had only read one book before age 25. It was a fiction book. Since that time, I have read or listened to hundreds of books, and all but two were non-fiction educational books. The two fiction books were "Atlas Shrugged" and "The Fountainhead," by the same author. I have read or listened to both three times. They are fiction but are based on the author's views of capitalism and her view of the wrong direction that our society is going, which is away from capitalism and toward socialism. I would suggest this book to anyone who wants to learn. Ayn Rand, the author, also wrote non-fiction books, including "Capitalism," but I will warn you that it is a tough read. Good, but tough.

In addition to Ayn Rand's books, I like Garrett Gunderson's books "Killing Sacred Cows," "The Money Tree," and "The Financial Freedom Mastery Course." Other important books to read include; "Secrets of the Millionaire Mind" by T. Harv Eker, "Rich Dad, Poor Dad" by Robert Kiyosaki, "The Millionaire Next Door" by Thomas Stanley, "Financial Peace" by Dave Ramsey, "12 Months to $1 Million" by Ryan Daniel Moran, and "The Art of the Deal" by Donald Trump.

There are plenty of other really good educational books, but these are a great start. Read as much as you can as quickly as you can and take in as much as you can. Call me and let's discuss what you have learned!

There is one other book that is more important than all of these noted previously and that is The Bible. I have and will reread all of the books listed. The Bible is one that I read annually. My goal is to read or listen to the entire Bible every five years, but the New Testament every year. I take six months and read 10 to 15 minutes daily. I am currently trying to read either the New Testament or the entire Bible rotating each year.

In order to do all of these things and then grow businesses, I must really have a schedule in place each day to get things accomplished. I do not always get all of this in each day, but I have the goals set and hit them as much as possible. I obviously feel that it is important to have a list of tasks daily to help me stay on track to grow my wealths, which includes education.

## FINANCIAL WEALTH

FINANCIAL WEALTH SHOULD BE THE least important of the five wealths, but it is necessary to provide for yourself or your family and to be able to help others.

Money is not the root of all evil, but worshipping money is the root of all evil. In my perspective, money is a means to help us do good things.

Dave Ramsey would say and has said that there are three things you can do with money. One can buy fun and happiness by going on a vacation, watching a movie, or going to a sporting event. One can invest money to make more money. And finally, one can give it away. We get the most satisfaction and joy out of giving money away and helping others. So, my goal is to make as much as I can by investing to enjoy life and give as much away as possible.

## WHY SPIRITUALITY FIRST

I'M NOT HERE TO PREACH. But I will say this— the foundation of my financial success is due in large part to my spiritual beliefs and practice. I believe that my faith gives me freedom. A freedom that can only come from the belief in a higher power.

For me, that's God. My faith gives me comfort that there is an afterlife and helps us through the mourning process of lost loved ones, by knowing that I will see them again one day in the afterlife. I can view things I do here and now through a different lens than if I did not have the faith that I have.

Believing gives me the freedom to live a life of joy and love. Believing gives me an explanation of the creation of this beautiful world we live in. Believing allows me the opportunity to use what I have been given, but also an understanding that what I've been given will not leave with me at the end of this life.

That said, this is my perspective. Everyone has their own opinion and that's to be respected. I hope that each of you has come to know and have a spiritual practice. There will be times in life, especially in your teen years, through high school and college that you may push away, question, try to overthink, or out-think faith.

I like to believe that faith is a belief in infinite love and that love can help us find our way through life. I also just hope you have a good basic foundation and belief, so that any paths you take in the wrong direction, you will find your way back.

## WHEN THE CHIPS MIGHT SEEM DOWN FOR OTHERS

THERE WERE MULTIPLE TIMES WHEN money was tight on deals that we were doing. Tight to the point that most would not have done the deals. Most would have felt that they were too risky, which has just not been an issue for us. I believe that religion and spirituality really help to provide a life of abundance and keep scarcity at bay for our family.

As any spiritual practitioner, I believe that we are always moving toward or away from our faith. We sometimes let other parts of our lives become higher priorities. We have to recognize this and re-prioritize at times.

I believe successful people and successful companies can contribute a large amount of success on the basis of being good and moral people who want to do good for others. People who want to provide value to clients, customers, friends, and family. The want/urge/need to be good and moral, I feel comes from a solid foundation in their religion and spirituality. Sure there are a few that are successful in some ways that may have gotten success from actions and intentions that may not be good or moral, but I would like to think that they are a small and hopefully insignificant group.

With regards to spirituality, I have noted and feel that it is the foundation for all the wealths and our levels of success in each wealth. I can say that for me personally, I can look back and note that the times when I feel I have been "hitting on all cylinders" or just feeling my most successful is when I have been really focused on each of the wealths and making all a priority with spirituality at the top of that list.

Additionally, I look back and remember times when I felt I was stuck or just not accomplishing things I wanted to accomplish. When I realized this, I would make needed changes to get my five wealths aligned with spirituality as the basis and things would start moving again for me.

It feels good and is productive to put out fires and complete tasks, which is why it is easy to get stuck in that frame of mind forever. But for me, I know that I can be much more successful when I take time each morning to dedicate to my personal growth in the five wealths, then additionally make a list of daily tasks, and weekly, monthly, and long-term goals. Then I am prepared and have the playbook and map to accomplish putting out those small fires (mostly through delegating to others) while staying focused on the big picture and growing my wealths. Another book that is helpful and related to this topic is "The Miracle Morning" by Hal Elrod.

I believe that most of us have times of ebbs and flows with different topics or mindsets rising to the top of our priority list. We also have breaks and vacations where we change up our routines. There will be different mixes of breaks and changes in routines for different people. There is no "one size fits all" for any of this.

One can be successful and really accomplish great wealth in each of these independently of the other, but the goal should be to become wealthy in all five.

If you want to be wealthy in all five, I believe that you have to have spiritual wealth at the top of the list. One can be smart, healthy, rich, and have great relationships, but in my view, will never be fully whole or be fulfilled in life without a relationship with a higher power. That person could look happy and be happy on paper or on social media, but they will not be one-hundred percent fulfilled.

Additionally, spiritual wealth automatically should put one in a great position with morals and how we deal with others in our society. Having good morals and integrity is important to our relationship wealth and business for financial wealth.

## BEING SUCCESSFUL IN THE 5 WEALTHS

BEING SUCCESSFUL IN THE FIVE wealths is not easy, but it is not hard either. It's a mindset—a way of life. One must make the decision to pursue all of the wealths. One can achieve just one or three, but true ultimate wealth and joy are obtained only when all five wealths are achieved.

An example of ultimate wealth or success in the five wealths would be as follows. A person that has a vision of where they want to be toward the end of their life. They want to be financially free. They never want to retire or they want to retire now no matter their age and enjoy life while being productive.

They do not need a budget because they make more than they ever need. They are positive, grateful, and joyful. They know where they want to be and are on the path to get there. They do not have to work for someone or on any schedule.

They can freely give because they have the means to do so. They love what they do and as such, leaving work at 65 or any age is not the main goal. Rather they want to continue doing what they love. They have the time to exercise as much as they want daily. They enjoy and spend much of their time educating themselves through reading, lectures, and conventions.

They can dedicate hours, days, and even weeks to mission trips, local aid, food banks, and any goodwill to those in need. They have the time to work on the five wealths whenever they feel like doing so. They can go on family nights or date nights every night if they want. This is what having ultimate wealth is all about.

If you work toward these five wealths, you will be putting the most important things first in your life.

## JOY IS A NECESSITY, NOT AN ACCESSORY

Now, IF WE WERE WRITING a recipe for a successful and joy-filled life, we would start with the base ingredient, which comes from the basis of my belief in love (joy). I believe that we are born with joy in our hearts and we find ways to remove joy. We are born with joy, but the ways of society complicate our lives and can take away our joy.

We can make decisions and put ourselves in positions to be joyful.

We can have this down pat and over time we let other thoughts and actions pull us away from this basic foundation. We look up and we are off track, we are unhappy, we are struggling in some aspect of our lives, and we have to realize that we need to get this foundation back in place before moving forward again.

It is important for us to understand that love and joy are imperative in our lives. We need to get this down first before taking any other step.

## CHALLENGE TO YOU

I'VE PRIORITIZED THE FIVE WEALTHS for a working person. In high school, college, and your early 20s, though, I'd prioritize it differently, by putting relationship wealth first. This is the time when you have the most access to meeting friends, experimenting with jobs and internships and a volume of people and interests. I suggest you take full advantage of that now, realizing it will shift down the road. Make friends. Keep in touch with your classmates and people with shared interests. Get to know people socially while you have the most time, energy, and interest in doing so.

# SMART GOALS + SMARTER PLANS

I wanted to propose to your mom in an extraordinary way.

My SMART goal [specific, measurable, achievable, relevant, timely], even though I didn't call it that at the time, was to propose on the beach in Destin, Florida, after a nice dinner at the nicest restaurant, and to do it in twelve months time.

First and foremost, I wanted to show Mom how important she was to me and demonstrate my love for her by doing something exceptional that should have been beyond my means at that time. Secondly, I wanted to do something bigger and better than almost anyone at my age and financial capacity had or will ever do, which was done by setting a goal and well-thought-out plans.

This was an achievable goal, but there were hurdles. By giving myself twelve months to work on it, I was able to add to my plans and come up with more exciting additions for the night. I will not bore you with all the planning and actions over the twelve months, but I will give you the way the night unfolded. You can then understand that there had to have been goals and plans to make it happen.

- **Three months out**—I met my mom to buy an engagement ring.
- **Ten days out**—I made reservations for the restaurant, a limousine, and flowers with precisely scripted instructions. Everyone involved was on board, and so kind.
- **Four days out**—I called Mom's dad and set up a meeting with him.
- **Three days out**—I drove an hour to meet Mom's dad in his office. I asked if I could marry his daughter and if he would be ok if we flew in a small Cessna plane down to the beach.

I had a friend in my fraternity whose dad owned a company that sold private planes, my friend had a pilot's license and kept a Cessna at the small airport in our college town. My friend talked his dad into allowing him to fly us to Florida to get in his needed flying hours if I would pay for the fuel. Fuel is not cheap and if I had not planned and figured this out months before, I would not have had the money. But because I planned it out, I knew the cost of the fuel and saved the money from one of my jobs after school that year.

Her dad said yes to both and I drove back before my afternoon lab.

## THE NIGHT BEFORE

I HAD ALREADY ASKED MOM a week ahead of time to go out that night and I had a surprise. That night before I told her that two friends had asked if she and I wanted to go up in this guy's plane, fly around for an hour or so, and then land back where we started. I also told her to wear something nice, because we would go straight to a dinner reservation after we flew. I asked my roommate if he wanted to go so that our pilot friend would not have to wait by himself.

## PROPOSAL DAY

**3:00**—I showered and duct-taped the engagement ring to my stomach. I knew that I would be in and out and up and down and did not want the ring, which was the most expensive thing I had owned at that point in my life, bouncing around in my pocket. I could not keep it in the box because that would've been obvious. I had a run-through with the ring a few hours a couple of days before to make sure it would work.

**4:00**—Mom and I drove to the local county airport. Neither of us had ever been on a small plane. So, this was our first private flight. When we arrived, our pilot friend gave Mom a single long-stem red rose—part of my plan.

**4:15**—we were up and flying. It was exciting for the three of us guys because they knew what we were doing and where we were going. Mom still thought we were flying around a bit and then landing where we started. There were a few times that airport control towers would have to give permission to enter and leave airspace. We all had on headsets, so as we got further away, the pilot would turn my and mom's headsets off before talking to air traffic controllers.

**5:30**—we descend through clouds to see the ocean. Mom remarks at how big and wide the Mississippi River looks, as that was the closest body of water where we took off. I broke the news that it was actually the Gulf of Mexico and that this was actually the surprise that I was taking her to dinner, but in Florida.

**5:45**—we land at the airport in Florida. As we come to a stop, a limo pulls up to the plane. The driver held the door for Mom with one hand and handed her a single red long-stem rose with his other hand. As we sat down in the limo, she found five more long-stem red roses—now at seven in total. The dinner destination was still a surprise.

**6:00**—we pull into the restaurant, which was across the street, but less than fifty or so yards from the beach. The limo driver opened the door and handed Mom another rose.

**6:01**—as we walk into the restaurant, the hostess opens the door, expecting us, and hands Mom another rose. She shows us straight to our table, where a vase with one long-stem red rose stands in the center.

**7:15**—we finish a wonderful dinner and I ask her if she wants to go walk down the beach since we were right there. The hostess is standing at the door as we are leaving with two more roses, of which she gives one to each of us.

**7:18**—we begin walking down the beach. I spend five minutes or so trying to untape the ring from my skin without being noticed.

**7:30**—we are ten to fifteen minutes into this walk on the beach. It is dark, but the full moon provides plenty of light along with lighting from buildings and businesses on the beach. I stop and hand Mom my rose, the twelfth. That is when I got down on a knee and asked her to marry me.

The rest, as they say, is history. We got back on the plane and back to school by 10:00 that night.

This was not as hard as buying or starting a business of course, but it shows you what cool moments you can create in your life by thinking ahead, setting an ultimate goal, then making plans and hitting mini-goals to achieve something that could not have been accomplished otherwise.

## BEING PURPOSEFUL ON YOUR PATH

JUST LIKE THIS PROPOSAL, BEING purposeful on the path to the five wealths also means setting goals and planning. Where most people fail before they even begin is in making—or not—their goals and plans. They might not even understand that they have to have goals and plans and if they do understand that, they don't know how to properly create and structure them. Goal setting, unfortunately, is not a standard requirement in schools like trigonometry. Yet.

## THE OFFICIAL DEFINITION

SMART IS THE ACRONYM FOR Specific, Measurable, Attainable, Relevant, and Timely. The concept was developed by George Doran, Arthur Miller, and James Cunningham in 1981 as a results-focused protocol.

I was often doing some form of SMART goals, even before I knew what they were, and you likely have been, too. With mom being a dentist and us building and buying practices, it wasn't until we were growing the first dental practice group that I formally learned the SMART structure, and when I did, I was able to quickly build on my previous goal-setting wins, just as you will, too. I've never failed with SMART goals, but I have failed or taken longer to reach a goal when I pursued something with undefined parameters or that was just too broad.

The original concept from 1981 has received some criticism due to the absence of process, but I've made it work for me because I've made my own process. I pair the written goals with ninja-level planning: tasks, plans, and mini-goals. In this way, I work through the process to get to the expected end result.

I like to sometimes shoot for goals so high that if I achieve 10% of that goal, then I will be much more successful than most would expect—that's what works for me. Others may have more success setting and attaining each goal as they go, building confidence with each victory.

## WHEN A GOAL IS ACTUALLY A HURDLE

Many times we think we are setting goals, but instead, we are making hurdles for ourselves. Meaning, that the goal is low enough that we do not strive for as much as we truly can obtain (i.e., I'm going to run a 5K vs a half marathon. If we strive for the half marathon, we will most likely hit the 5K on the way regardless of whether we make it to the half marathon).

Consistently setting and reviewing goals and plans is how I got from $300,000 in debt to a path to surpass $300,000,000 in financial wealth. One major note - I have probably hit 50% of my goals, but the misses have still been so far ahead of where I would have been without a goal. I would note that I hit almost all of my goals the older I get and the more goals I set. There are also many of my goals that I have way overshot, meaning I've possibly doubled or tripled my goal.

Working toward a goal will help you to get better and having no goals will keep you from getting better. Missing a goal has better results than not moving or growing at all.

## PAST GOALS

As a kid, I wanted to play baseball in college and then be a Major League Baseball player. As a young teen, I wanted to be a musician with a record deal on a major label by 24. At 18, I wanted to be an optometrist. Now at 47, I can say that I'm glad that I did not reach those three goals. I am much happier and wealthier where I am now than I ever could have been with those three goals, but they did help me to get where I am today.

This shows the importance of having a goal and pursuing it. You can always change it. What it teaches you is how to move forward and learn a ton in the process. When you push yourself to achieve something, you naturally learn about yourself and what helps you be successful in your individual process.

## EVOLUTION OF GOALS

IN MY EARLY LIFE, I wanted to be a pro baseball player, then a musician. At age 21, I wanted to marry your mom. At age 27, I decided I wanted to own a construction company and did start a construction company, while still working on music.

At age 28, your mom and I decided together that we wanted to start a family. This decision helped me to move away from the music goal. We knew that the life of a musician was hard on a family unit. At age 30, we decided to build and start a dental practice.

Each year after, we wanted and built, started, or purchased at least one business or property. Everything we did was due to a goal being set and accomplished or just missed but also prepared us for the next goal and accomplishment. Just as the saying goes "You must learn to crawl before you walk," you must learn and grow from smaller jobs, businesses, and real estate deals before doing bigger deals.

My plan now is to have at minimum 400 properties, write ten or more books, plus 25 to 30 songs, and own two restaurant chains of 150 plus locations each in my lifetime. I also plan to get and keep defined muscles and be in great shape for the next 30 years, which takes regular workouts 5 days a week.

These are lofty goals, but I do know that they are attainable with the right plans in place. I would've considered this a pipe dream 10 years ago. But I would have also considered what we currently have as a pipe dream 20 years ago.

## SUCCESS DIFFERENTIATORS

I GIVE YOU THIS INFORMATION to say that nothing can hold you back. However, our mindset is the difference between wanting and doing. You have to be able to take the first step and then you can take one step at a time until you have accomplished what was once considered a pipe dream to yourself.

This "model" is pretty common and nothing that I am doing differently than any other successful company or business. It is more a matter of setting the goals with the SMART aspects, staying on track, and following through that makes them work. This means that mini-goals and tasks must be set and performed to get to be successful. It's not a "set it and forget it" kind of thing.

A SMART goal may be on a ten-year timeline, however, in order to achieve that goal, it's necessary to hit annual, quarterly, monthly, weekly, and daily SMART goals in the process. Daily tasks may need to be achieved as well.

Some who are very successful, may not write or even think about these different goals, but they are going through a similar process or have those that work for them working through some process to get the desired results. It is just easier for me to write and work through tasks and mini-goals to hit SMART goals and have success. I happen to believe that your odds of reaching success are higher when doing it this way, though you may find some ways to tweak the recipe for what works best for you. We are always looking one, five, ten, and twenty years out.

## BEACH HOUSE EXAMPLE

THE FIRST PIECE OF THE puzzle that many people miss is the timeframe. Many people are looking only at the short term: tomorrow, this week, this month, this year. The magic is in longer-term planning—we can do much more with much less effort.

We must break the thought of immediate response and gratification and train ourselves to think longer term. This can be two, five, ten, twenty, or forty years. As an example, let's set a goal of owning a beach house in Florida. Having a waterfront property could be a goal of a majority of people, and that is exactly how they would frame the goal, too.

Great and fun idea, but the problem here is that the person who sets this "goal" today will say the same thing in ten, twenty, and thirty years from now. The vast majority of people won't attain it. Why? Lack of action in turning their idea into a reality: no SMART goals—no specificity, no measurement, maybe it is thought to be achievable, but no defined relevance to their life, no timeline, and worst: no planning. How will you actually achieve anything with that framework? Answer: you probably won't.

But you could. Here's how:

Define the goal in SMART terms and make a plan. Let's say you want a $2 million oceanfront home in Santa Rosa Beach, Florida, specifically 30A, in exactly 20 years from today. This may sound crazy or out of reach, but please stay with me. I promise you, there is a path there. This is an oversimplified example, not taking inflation and all financials into account, but this goal hits all of the requirements of a SMART goal. The only catch is whether it is or is not attainable. I would say, with the proper mindset that it is attainable for anyone.

We will need 20% down or $400,000 and will need to be able to make mortgage payments of around $10,500 per month after purchase. This means that we need to save $1,700 per month for the down payment and then have an annual income between $250,000 and $300,000 per year at the time of purchase unless we rent it when we are not using it. We can buy assets that will give us both the $1,700 average per month over the twenty years and produce between $250,000 and $300,000 annually.

Now that we have a SMART goal, we can begin planning. Most would say that this is a bit over the top, but I include a business plan format in my plans, which includes:

1) An overview of the business and in this case that is a goal that we want to obtain.
2) A description of the business, its history, how it works, and in this case, how the goal can be attained, growth plans, and long and short-term goals. It also includes the plan for the company's growth, along with long-term and

short-term goals. For our goals, we can look at how we plan to grow to achieve the goal and how the long-term and short-term goals will be our mini-goals.

3) Products and Services, for this example, it's more about the assets we will need to obtain to produce the money.
4) Market analysis, for this, it's more about justifying our assets that we will purchase and then showing how we can feasibly get to needed revenue.
5) Strategy and implementation, this will add the layers of plans needed.
6) The organization and management team, for us will be laying out the team of players that we will need to obtain and retain the asset and keep the asset productive.
7) The financial plan and projections, for us will be looking at the potential asset or assets and figuring out what we need to do to obtain those assets. Additionally, we will have projections for revenue from those assets which will get us the needed revenue.

Part of planning will be mini-goals and then a business plan for each mini-goal. Back to our example, if we need $400,000 for that down payment in twenty years and we need $250,000 to $300,000 annual income in the twentieth year, then we might need to have multiple assets to hit that ultimate goal.

Let's say we buy and rent a residential house that produces a net of $15,000 per year, we might need seventeen of these rental properties by the twentieth year. We will need a business plan of sorts for each one. This may sound daunting, but remember: it's more than twenty years. As a kindergartner, you likely weren't thinking about buying yourself a car with your allowance or your lemonade stand money.

## BUT, DEE, I CAN'T!! NO WAY!

Yes, this is a lofty goal, no doubt. It is attainable for those who have the drive, persistence, and mindset. Stay curious, and stay with me here. Consider that the first 10 years may be very slow, $1k to $5k savings. Then, the last 10 years will need to be closer to $35k to $40k in savings. This may seem nearly insane right now, but my stance is that this is doable for anyone, if they plan it out correctly and use the tools in this book.

It will not work for those who take their eye off the goal and go buy consumer debt products over the next 20 years. So, with proper steps taken—hurdle number one the $400k down payment: check!

Hurdle number two is the $12k monthly note. This may seem harder and will be harder if you think about it as something you want to do tomorrow or even next year. Please listen very closely, if you do nothing—if you do not plan this out—you will be in exactly the same place in 20 years. With the majority. Lamenting about the beach house you want instead of the beach house you're on your way to having.

But goals and plans are part of the secret sauce, as well as backing into your goal 20 years from now. Backing into the goal is knowing you will need $12k of extra money monthly or $144k annually in 20 years. This means you will need to plan to have a second, third, or fourth stream of income in that timeframe. This is playing the long game.

You will have your primary income to cover your living expenses and lifestyle. These additional streams of income could be multiple rental houses, a business or two, or other passive income investments.

Don't miss the bigger picture here. Let's say you fail at your 20-year goal and only save half of the $400k or only have passive income to cover half or $6k per month. With this failure, you have achieved THIS GREAT HIDDEN SECRET that I am trying to preach in this chapter about goals and tasks. If you did not set and take action on the beach house goal, then you would not have $200k and $6k of monthly passive income!

Now, at the time of your deadline with $200k saved and $6k passive income you have a choice. You downsize in location or size of a beach house OR you extend your time horizon by 5 or 10 years. Most who understand and adopt this book will be able to double their wealth in 10 years and many will double it in 5 years.

If you have read this and think "That is impossible" or "I can't do that," then this book has not succeeded.

If you feel that it is too big of a goal, it's because you have not changed your mindset. You have not given proper thought to the SMART goal and the long-term plan. Maybe this is just not something you care to attempt and feel it is too much stress for you. I would suggest reading this book every year or two and one of the passes you may just have that shift in your mind. I promise that it is doable for almost anyone with the right recipe and—mindset!

## STARTING FROM SCRATCH

Your mom and I started from scratch. Less than scratch, actually, given our debt, initially. We purchased an entity (either a business or a property) every year for ten years. Then we have purchased multiples every year after the first ten years, so it is very doable. It is all about breaking it down and planning it out properly.

Another part of planning is to have a timeline for every step. This timeline will begin now and end at the ultimate goal, which in our example is twenty years. The timeline will have all mini-goals as well as important dates for steps in our plans. In our example, we are using real estate and if we want to make $15,000 per year the first year, we will need to determine what type of real estate property will give us that type of return.

## FINAL THOUGHTS

The next ingredients for this great, joy-filled, and successful aspect in every part of one's life are ultimate goals, priorities, mini-goals, plans, and then monthly, weekly, and daily tasks to achieve these ultimate goals.

One can be successful and one can have a busy life, but it is almost impossible for one to attain a high level of wealth and be truly successful without goals, priorities, plans, and tasks. Furthermore, no matter where one is in their life, they can achieve great wealth in every aspect of life and be filled with love and joy if they follow this recipe.

I want you to learn this deeper than I did, earlier than I did. Even with proposing to your mom, I'm just now able to look back and see how that type of thinking has helped me be successful throughout my life.

If I'd had this book or information and the capacity to understand this concept alone at age 18, I would be in much better shape, be more educated in business, more connected, and in general, much further along in all the wealths.

One specific example is if I had planned out my path with owning a construction business, flipping houses, and knew where I wanted that to go, I believe that could've been a very lucrative business for me. Instead, I did not have a solid plan. So, I ended up buying and flipping one house, remodeling the house we lived in, doing three other remodeling jobs, and then walking away from that business with very little to show for it. With the proper goals and plans, I could have built that business into a multi-million dollar company.

## 📍 CHALLENGE TO YOU

THINK OF A FINANCIAL GOAL you want to accomplish or a type of property you'd like to purchase—something big, that stretches you. Write it down in the SMART format: specific, measurable, attainable, relevant, and time-based. Write it in a paper notebook (preferred) or a digital format. Think about the timeframe—consider whether it's three, six, or nine months, or one, three or five years, or more. Write it all down.

Then, take a crack at your plan. Just a first draft, you're not committing to anything. Write a messy page, even. Cut your timeframe in half, and think about what has to happen at that halfway mark. Do the same for the one-quarter mark and the three-quarter mark. What other details can you fill in? Key mile-markers you need to hit? Key tasks you need to do? Write it all down. Then, find a mentor—someone who's done it or things like it—and ask if they'd be willing to have a conversation with you. Bet they will. Review your plan.

Include in your plans to revisit this book every year or two, especially if the concepts sound as foreign and far off as intergalactic space travel. I promise you, many have done it—I have done it—and you can, too.

For your own personal fun and enjoyment, save your goals and plans. It is great to look back at a twenty-year goal and see the difference after the twenty years.

# THE PSYCHOLOGY OF MINDSET: ABUNDANCE VS SCARCITY

Mom and I taught a wealth class through our church to a small group of young adults. One of the students, Jacob, was really interested in the subject and asked to meet me separately to understand and discuss how he could apply these concepts to his current job at a large construction company.

He wanted to change his direction and start down a new path in his career. I helped him to see that there were decisions and plans that could help him minimize his concerns, one of which was scarce thinking. I explained to him that there was minimal upfront cost, he was single at the time, and he would have his first job to fall back on if the business failed.

With us opening his mind to bigger possibilities, he noticed that while working for the large construction company, there was a niche in hanging doors that most contractors did not like doing. In construction, there are many sub-contracting businesses like plumbers, electricians, framers, and many others.

Jacob noticed that hanging doors did not fall under any sub-contracting business. It wasn't a hard thing to do, but it did take special tools and was kind of a pain if you were doing one-offs. General contractors didn't like doing it because it took extra time and they weren't efficient at it. Therefore, it ultimately costs them money. Jacob, however, was good at it and noticed different contractors in his company asking him to hang doors for them. So, Jacob worked with me on coming up with a plan to start his own business doing this as a sub-contractor.

Outside of minimizing his risk, I worked with Jacob on abundant thinking and what his future could look like. Two years earlier, he was making $17 to $20 per hour and was working 40 hours a week clocking in and out daily on someone else's schedule. Fast forward, he has a very successful business with four employees which has provided him with 5 to 10X more income, freedom to be on his own schedule and not someone else's, and really put him on a projection to be financially independent.

But more importantly, he has a much more abundant mindset. He has made time to do more things he enjoys. He has since gotten married and went to Europe for a honeymoon, which he could not have done before. He is in his twenties and has much more life ahead of him, and his abundance mindset will make that life much more joyful. He is currently working on starting a second business.

## THE COMMON DEFAULT

SCARCITY THINKING IS A COMMON default. At a young age, society grooms us with a scarcity mindset. The message is that there's only so much money in the world: the rich get richer and the poor get poorer and if you make money, someone has to give up or lose money.

Scarcity is a "glass half empty" mindset. It evokes worry, fear, and trepidation. Worried, afraid, and scared that something bad might happen, that something cannot get done, or that others will think something.

My mindset earlier in life was what was instilled in me through my parents and the people around me. We all were somewhat taught to have a scarcity mindset. Stay within the rules or you can get hurt. Save your money, stay on a budget, follow the norm, etc. are all a form of scarcity mindset passed down from generation to generation.

Scarcity is what kills our opportunities to reach goals. Scarcity mindsets think "There is one dollar in the room and you or I can have it, so one wins and the other loses." This is looking at the dollar as the value or the object that is wanted or needed.

## SCARCITY IN A BUSINESS

IN THE CONTEXT OF RUNNING a business that is struggling, many leaders go straight to scarcity thinking and slash expenses. They stop spending money that was previously helping them be successful. They might stop marketing, cut back on supplies, or cut payroll by firing employees or reducing hours.

I know of a dental company that had such a scarce business mindset that they:

1) provided 1 roll of toilet paper per week to their staff of six women. The staff was told if they ran out, they would have to bring their own or go without.
2) told their staff to wear one pair of gloves and face mask all day, which was against OSHA standards.
3) cut back cleaning crew and employee hours.

These are perfect examples of scarce thinking. Consider the effect the toilet paper had on the staff's positive and productive actions. Consider the impact it could have if OSHA or patients found out they were not as sanitary with gloves and masks as they should have been. Consider the effect of a dirty-looking office from below-standard cleaning. And finally, consider the impact of less hospitality and customer service provided with half the staff that was the standard.

This is the type of business that Mom and I look at—ones that have some of these scarcity issues. We like to invest in them because turning them around is relatively easy with a moderate investment of money.

I am more risk-tolerant than anyone I know. I do not take unnecessary risks, but I feel less stress and worry over some risks than someone in a scarcity mindset. Additionally, I came from very little and understand that money is not what brings me joy; therefore, I am not as worried about risk as one who gets their worth from money or one who feels that money is the root of their joy.

## THE ABUNDANCE MINDSET

AN ABUNDANCE MINDSET IS HAVING an outlook on life with a positive spin: "glass half-full," optimism, finding ways to win, ways to accomplish, and ways to get things done. Being happy and joyful is a result of abundance thinking.

An abundance mindset is the opposite of a scarcity mindset: it's that money is not finite, but infinite. Abundance sees that you can take that dollar and use it to buy my candy bar. Then I have the dollar and use it to buy your soda. Then you use the dollar to use my phone for ten minutes. Now I have the dollar. And this can go on forever. This example is putting the value in goods and services and the dollar is just a means covering a traded good or service.

On a macro scale, one can use a large amount of money, but that money gets moved and used many times. This is the velocity in money and allows multiple people to use the same money over and over, which shows that everyone can win instead of one winner and one loser.

I thought about abundance and scarcity like anyone else probably would when I first heard and thought about it 20 years ago. My thought was I should be positive and not negative thinking and I should have an open mind and not a closed mind. However, when I focused on this concept it really clicked for me that this thinking has a much deeper impact on our success in life and in each of the wealths.

Abundance and scarcity are mindsets and are not specific to money only. Living in scarcity, we see people mad and afraid. Afraid to fly, afraid to travel, afraid to take a chance, afraid to talk to someone, afraid that someone will see them as "not perfect," afraid of so many things. Mad that they don't have what others have, mad that they did not get picked for this or recognized for that, and this list can go on and on.

Living in abundance is just the opposite. It's being excited, joyful, looking forward, excited at possibilities, open to the chance of making something happen or making a change, and on that list goes. Abundance is a mindset of gratitude, forgiveness, and joy. The glass is half full. Abundance is finding joy in giving a gift, doing something for others, and making others happy. Love is abundant and living a loving life is abundant. We have to remember this ourselves sometimes when we let society draw us into scarcity.

A list of scarcity vs abundance examples that can help you shift into the right mindset:

| SCARCITY | ABUNDANCE |
| :---: | :---: |
| Criticize | Compliment |
| Take credit | Give credit to others |
| Entitlement | Gratitude |

| SCARCITY | ABUNDANCE |
|---|---|
| Holding a grudge | Forgiving |
| Know it all | Open to learning |
| Letting the world around guide | Setting goals and planning |
| Exude anger | Exude joy |
| Lie around | Exercise |
| Blame others | Accept responsibility |
| Fear change | Accept change |
| Watch TV or social media | Read books to learn |
| Worry | Calm |

It's important to recognize when you are slipping into scarcity and work to get back into abundance.

If we base our lives on love and realize that this life is simply a place in time with time being eternal, then we have a different outlook and can understand and live in abundance. This is closely linked with one's spiritual practice.

## ABUNDANCE AND RISK TOLERANCE

WHEN IT COMES TO MONEY and scarcity vs abundance, there is a huge difference in risk tolerance when you have an abundant mindset. For example, my own tolerance to risk is much higher due to my abundance mindset combined with my spiritual practice.

See, I believe that I had nothing when I came into this world and will leave this world with nothing. I have money and can be a steward of that money. As long as I view money as a means to help others and not allow money to become a "god" or something I give all my time and energy to, then this mindset is freeing. I then don't really care if I have a mountain of money or hardly any money at all. My mindset is that I can have millions today and I will be happy tomorrow, even if I lost all of my money.

This doesn't mean that I am overly risky or careless in business, but instead have this amazing freedom to strive for more without a fear of losing. I can do deals worth millions of dollars and do not lose sleep like others.

This is not to say that I haven't had many sleepless nights in my life, but as I have learned to live in this mindset, I've dramatically decreased my nights of tossing and turning. I still find myself worrying, but quickly recognize it and make that mental change. It is freeing and joyful to be able to do that, which is why it's so important to me to educate you about this freedom.

My advice is to keep your thinking and actions somewhere between conservative and aggressive or between a spender and a miser. Moderation is key. Remember life is a marathon and not a sprint, and there's a reason I'm coaching you for the long game.

## THE GAP BETWEEN PROCESSING AND ACTION

MUCH LIKE PACKAGING THE FIVE wealths together, I only started thinking seriously about the layer of abundance thinking many years after first hearing the concept. Combining it with the other concepts here supercharges their power. I had known and understood these concepts since the early 2000s but began making them a priority around 2016/2017. It's been said that sometimes we take ten years to come to a decision and then one month to take meaningful action on it.

This processing-to-action gap is a critical part of introducing these concepts to you earlier in life, so you can start processing them earlier, and put them in action earlier as well—in your early 20s, instead of like I did, in my late 30s.

## THE SYNERGY

THE FIVE WEALTHS, PLUS GOAL setting and action planning, along with an abundance mindset are synergistic. Everything gets simpler and easier the more these concepts are used together. Likewise, the freedom gained from spiritual wealth makes it so much easier to increase abundant thinking.

I feel that the biggest change in abundance for me was when I realized that having and keeping a tight budget was putting me in a scarcity thought process. I realized that working to increase my income led me to a more abundant mindset than trying to cut my expenses to stay within a budget.

In both examples of fights with my dad and big debt in businesses, I did not have as much of an abundant mindset as I would now. And if I were in those situations again with my current abundant mindset, I know that I would not have had the stress related to each.

I can say that my spiritual beliefs were a great help in cultivating an abundant mindset. Because I have true faith in God, I have this liberating feeling that ultimately things will work out. Just that thought helps to push me in the direction of an abundant mindset.

## SLOW + STEADY DENTAL BUILD

WE ARE BEING SOLD ALL kinds of get-rich schemes, but none of them work—and I proved that in both a positive and negative way with our dental practices.

When we were starting out, Mom and I built the first practice and waited to see results before starting another practice. After two years, we opened a second practice, and after two more years—year four now—we opened our third practice.

After the third, we opened one practice per year for six more years. When we had eight practices doing really well, we received an offer that we could not refuse and sold those practices. In my mind, we knew the business of dentistry well. I could and did teach others the business side of dentistry. We had a non-compete for two years in our area, so within a year of selling the eight practices, we purchased three practices in another state. Then within six months, we purchased three more in that state.

All of these practices in the new state were purchased like many of the original eight practices, from older dentists wanting to retire. What we did not know at the time, was that it was much harder to find and hire new dentists in that state.

It was so difficult that we've since sold one practice to break even, sold another practice at a huge loss, and closed two practices with hundreds of thousands of dollars of loss.

If we had purchased one per year like we had previously done then we would have figured out the issue after two practices and not lost much if any money at all. Slow and steady growth helps you to "know the things you don't know." This was a lesson that has cost us over a million dollars. I have learned my lesson on moderation by slow and steady growth in business.

The takeaway: stay grounded and know that good growth does not happen overnight. In all aspects of your life, think about the extremes and try to find a middle ground. Have fun and enjoy life, but realize that you need to be balanced in your approach to having fun. Recognize any scarcity that begins creeping into your mind and quickly change it to an abundant mindset.

## HOW TO FIND THE SWEET SPOT

MY ADVICE WOULD BE TO keep an abundant mindset and find a good mentor. Run your abundant thinking goals by one or two mentors. Find someone who is in the field or has some background understanding of what you want to do and get their opinion. The goal here is to continue thinking abundantly and finding ways to lessen risk.

There is a sweet spot, but that sweet spot is a personal calculation. It's dictated by one's understanding of the goal and the risk involved. Again, we want to be pushing hard enough that we are failing and learning from our failures, but not in a way that will ruin our big dream goals and timeline. Some would call it educated or calculated risks. And this will change as you grow, develop, and are more educated in the things you are doing.

Like all the concepts we've discussed thus far, an abundance mindset is a process of awareness, practice, and trial and error to find your exact recipe.

## CHALLENGE TO YOU

START PAYING ATTENTION TO YOUR thoughts on money. Do they lean toward abundance or scarcity? Where and how can you shift your scarcity thoughts into abundance?

The hardest thing to understand when starting out in any business is being overly optimistic and not knowing what you don't know. A person who has done it before can help with both of these. My challenge to you is to get into the practice of talking to people 10-30 years older than you when making big life decisions such as job/career changes, investments, and risk-carrying activities. They can help you maximize your potential upside and minimize your risk.

# 7

# PRODUCTIVE, CONSUMPTIVE, DESTRUCTIVE—HOW YOU USE YOUR TIME

While I was a fan of both Ferris Bueller and Magnum PI, I was never a gearhead—nor did I have this affection for cars. In fact, I've always been against expensive cars. They depreciate.

Many people however, including our friends and neighbors, take pride in buying the most expensive car that they can afford right now. This means they own vehicles that are double or triple the cost of an average new vehicle.

As soon as they can afford a nicer car, they will then go and get that—a continual upgrade loop. Unfortunately, this practice and mindset carries over to many things in their lives and these things lead to ongoing, and in my opinion (which none of them have asked for!), unnecessary consumption and debt.

Since my focus is on productive, long-term thinking, and investments, I've consistently bought the average-priced vehicle that can get us from point A to point B. All but twice in my life,

I've bought used cars—not new. I then use that difference in what other people are spending to invest instead.

And while I never really had this love or affinity for exotic cars, I can appreciate the art of the look and lines, the horsepower and performance, and the value they hold—that's where my real interest began.

When considering investing my money into different types of assets, I usually put everything into a business or property. Yet every financial advisor I have talked to consistently noted my overweighted investing in real estate. This is usually because they want to make money on my investment into life insurance, mutual funds, stocks, or something that they can sell. I also hear people talk about storing money in other assets like gold and silver or even artwork.

Well, I don't really have a great appreciation for art, gold and silver are boring to me, so I turned my attention to exotic cars, which in my mind an exotic car is art on wheels. I can sit in these cars and even drive them from time to time, and they should hold their value. Meaning, that the right cars will increase in value over time. So, not the traditional "guy's" answer to "Why exotic cars?", yet that's my reason for exotic cars.

I plan to buy eight cars from $200,000 to $2,000,000 in value. My first was what I considered an entry-level car, but also one of the best-looking in my opinion—the 2004 Ferrari 360 Spider, with 5,000 miles on it.

The plan is to collect and let them be another form of income as they grow in value over a fifteen to thirty-year period. This is long-term and productive thinking that creates some enjoyment from time to time but hopefully ends in a productive investment.

If you are looking to get "the next best thing" right now, you may never have the money to buy anything that you really want later in life. This is the difference between a consumptive and productive mindset and instant gratification versus playing the long game.

## ABOUT THE CONCEPT

MANY ECONOMIC THEORISTS ANALYZE THE optimal amount of production versus the amount of consumption for business. I look at these same concepts in our life and specifically as it relates to our decisions and actions—what we are doing.

This concept categorizes our decisions and activities into three categories: productive, consumptive, or destructive. I use this line of thinking in combination with all five wealths and the other concepts in the book. Simply put, it helps me analyze and quantify my use of time and money to help me make sure I am maximizing the productivity of my time and money.

These concepts are broad and have been around forever. This is more about specifying how they are used. Garrett introduced me to making these concepts work together. I have just taken these concepts and used them with goals, schedules, and tasks to personalize them to work with my strengths and take them to another level. After recognizing, defining, and putting these concepts all together, I multiplied the results that I was getting—it made everything flow with remarkable ease.

For me, I need to really focus on productivity and planning or I easily veer into consumptive behavior and loosen the handle I have on my current goal, which sets me back.

I've gotten good at being productive with my time through daily schedules. I find that when I do not schedule my day, it becomes very consumptive. It really gets tough for me when I am traveling a lot. But the more specific I schedule, the more productive my results. It is easier to explain and recognize productivity in regard to financials.

## TIME APPLICATION OF CONCEPTS

WE WILL REALLY DRILL DOWN on productive, consumptive, and destructive living habits, as well as financial habits. Like the other concepts, this is a foundational element—a way of life and a mindset. It is also a great example of how life around us will provide the default way of living as consumptive or destructive if we do not consciously choose to be productive.

There are times in our lives when we are in and out of all three categories, but we should strive to be weighted heavily in the productive category. We also need a healthy amount of consumptive living. And finally, we want to totally stay away from destructive activities if possible. Let's define each from a daily perspective.

Productive activities are doing anything that helps you in the five wealths of life. Examples of productivity are exercising, educational reading or audio listening (non-fiction), spiritual, mental, and physical activities, helping others, doing any type of work that provides a good or service to others, any work that makes money legally, healthy eating, and growing relationships with family and friends are just a few. We cannot be productive all the time.

The most important principle to understand is that we want to be more productive than consumptive in our daily activities and with our lives in general. Taking a break and enjoying life is usually considered a consumptive activity. Going on a vacation is consumptive.

Consumptive activities do not help you advance in the five wealths of life, but give you breaks, provide enjoyment, reduce stress, and can help to reset and get you ready to get back to your productive activities. When I am watching TV, taking a nap, playing golf, baking a cake, or hunting, I am consuming or being consumptive.

Destructive activities hurt you as a person, impede your growth, and can hurt those around you. If I were to drink alcohol, do drugs, gamble, or do anything that can be addictive, that would be a destructive use of time.

We are all productive, consumptive, and sometimes destructive in our daily lives and in general over our lifetime. Being productive, an individual is growing, helping, and giving while being consumptive, an individual is using, taking, and sometimes hindering themselves and/or others. There is also rest, which can be either productive or consumptive. Getting a healthy eight hours of sleep is productive for mental and physical health. It is needed for us to be at our peak performance.

## HOW YOU USE IT

I HAVE ADOPTED THE PROCESS of using income from businesses and properties to reinvest in another business or property. I have heard some financially successful people who do not consume any active income but re-invest that active income into a passive income-producing investment. They can then use the passive income to purchase "fun things" which are most times consumptive. All of my income is passive, so I reinvest almost always. Reinvesting in properties and businesses is productive.

How much we are productive is a personal preference and practice. My take at this time in my life is to strive to be more than 50% productive. I personally want to have as high a percentage of productivity without burning out.

We feel better if we are doing productive things. We have a better attitude and have joy in our lives when we are more productive. Going for a walk or exercising is productive by helping us to be healthier and feel better.

I would consider going to dinner with my family both consumptive and productive. It is consumptive in that I am paying for that meal and someone else was productive and worked to cook the meal. It is productive in the way that I am adding value to my relationship with my family by spending time and talking. These examples should give a good idea of this mindset.

Setting long-term goals will help keep things in moderation. Trying to study for a test an hour before the test is not going to work out well while studying in small amounts over a week or two will produce much better results. Trying to gain or lose fifteen pounds in a week is unhealthy and destructive while making a plan and setting a goal to lose fifteen pounds over twelve months can be healthy and productive.

In general, our culture has a problem with overspending. We are outweighed with consumptive and destructive over a productive mindset. In the aspect of health, consuming more calories than one's daily needs than calories burned from exercise and daily activities makes a person consumptive.

On the flip side, being in alignment with the right amount of calories and exercise can make a person healthier and more productive. The majority of the U.S. population is overweight. I would also go as far as to note that the people you hang around, as well as, the shows and movies you watch, and the music you listen to can be destructive. It takes us in the opposite direction of productivity and being positive. It is not as bad as an addiction and can be easily turned around, but it can be destructive.

## FINANCE APPLICATION OF CONCEPTS

THE SECOND AND JUST AS important way of viewing these concepts is financially. Productive spending is spending on things that make us money, such as education, health, investments, businesses, real estate, etc. Borrowing debt for any of these productive spending activities is ok, but using cash would be better. One's personal house can be consumptive and productive.

A house is an appreciating asset which is productive. But I would caution that overspending on a house or buying a house that is too expensive can get into consumptive and maybe even borderline destructive. "Too expensive" would be more than 25% of your current income—and not the income you're going to make "after" you get that raise. Twenty-five percent as of now. Consumptive spending is spending money on things that do not make money but give us joy. Nice personal cars, most clothes, vacations and trips, restaurants and coffee shops are a few examples of consumptive spending. We should never use debt, credit cards, or loans with these, but cash only (cash being money you have on hand or in a checking or savings account). I will note that a car used for business and some clothes bought specifically for business could be considered productive.

Destructive spending is spending on things that do not make us money and hurt us. Alcohol, drugs, pornography, cigarettes, gambling—anything that can be categorized as an addiction is destructive. We do not want to spend any money (debt or cash) on destructive items or ways of living.

## MOVING TOWARD PRODUCTIVITY

THERE ARE MANY DIFFERENT THOUGHTS, frames of mind, and situations that can move us toward or hold us back from any accomplishment. It is important that you are actively being productive to reach any goal and accomplish any big plans. It is impossible to accomplish any goal or plan in a destructive state. So, the simple answer here is that destructive or too much of consumptive mindsets are what can hold you back from an accomplishment.

Sleeping for twelve hours, especially after you have been up too long doing something destructive, can then be consumptive. Being lazy is also consumptive.

Finally, destructive activities, such as overdrinking and alcoholism, drugs and drug addiction, gambling, pornography, and overindulging are things we want to stay away from altogether. Playing a video game for an hour or two is consumptive, but playing for hours on end gets destructive because it hinders one's mental growth.

Now the goal here is to be more productive than consumptive and not destructive at all. We all need to have downtime, which is consumptive. Playing a sport, hunting, fishing, watching TV, and reading fiction are all consumptive activities, but are ways to de-stress for many people. Exercising and reading a non-fiction "how-to" or educational book are examples of productive activities that are also de-stressors for many people.

If you are consuming all of the time, you cannot be a producer. Your production must outweigh consumption to have a wealthy life.

Similarly, most, who reach a certain level of success, buy a second home (a lake house, mountain home, or beach house). I have purchased six properties that are secondary homes in either beach or mountain properties. If they were strictly second homes, then they would be considered consumptive purchases. I purchased all of these properties and underwrote them (running a pro forma) to cover my costs and debt service (loan) through rent. I can rent these properties and use them from time to time personally. Then rents will help to pay off all debts, making these properties productive.

A good example of productive thinking and how it worked well for me is when I began writing this book. I had been wanting to write this book for a few years but never made the time to get started. It is easy for all of us to finish a regular day of work and then "veg out" the rest of the day until it is bedtime. Nothing wrong with a little downtime to rest and recharge. We all have different needs for rest with sleep or downtime. I need very little downtime, so anything over 30 to 60 minutes of downtime (watching TV) and I am being consumptive. I, like anyone else, go through ruts where I find myself not being productive.

If I don't schedule and task productivity, I default to consumption. Our purchases of properties and businesses make my daily workload very erratic. There are days and weeks when I am very busy trying to get deals done, while there are much slower days and weeks. It was one of these downtimes when I fell into a rut of being lazy or consumptive in my mind. At that time I made a conscious decision to make that time more productive and begin writing this book. What I had put off for a few years, I was able to do in about six months.

Personal success requires a productive mindset and an awareness and focus on productivity. Many people who struggle with success often struggle with being too consumptive, amongst other things. Most businesses are always working to get employees to have a more productive mindset and work ethic. As a business grows and more employees are hired, whether it is acknowledged or not, one of the most important jobs for operations managers is to find ways to encourage employees to work harder, which is really being more productive with their time.

## WHAT DOES THIS LOOK LIKE IN A DAILY SCHEDULE?

### Sample Teen Schedule with More Than 50% Productive Time

The rough breakdown here is approximately 6.5 hours of productive health for sleep, 6 hours productive for learning,

7.5 hours consumptive, and 4 hours of transition (also consumptive) for a total of 24 hours. Just as with the normal adult, weekends would be weighted heavily if not 100% of waking hours as consumptive.

A normal day for a teen would be as follows:

- **6:00 am to 6:40 am**—Wake and shower (productive for getting ready to go to school and learn to be productive)
- **6:40 am to 7:00 am**—Breakfast with family and get ready for school (productive relationship)
- **7:00 am to 7:45 am**—Commute to school (listening to music consumptive)
- **7:45 am to 2:30 pm**—School (productive for learning with a good dose of consumptive for talking to friends between classes, during classes, and lunch) (could also be productive for relationships)
- **2:30 pm to 4:00 pm** (productive for health with after-school activity)
- **4:00 pm to 4:30 pm** (consumptive with music and commuting home)
- **4:30 pm to 7:00 pm** (consumptive with music, social media, watching something)
- **7:00 pm to 7:30 pm** (productive for health with dinner and relationship)
- **7:30 pm to 11:30 pm** (consumptive with music, social media, watching something)
- **11:30 pm to 6:00 am** (sleep productive for health).

## Sample Adult Schedule with More Than 75% Productive Time

Here is a good example of a schedule that is more than 50% productive for an adult: health, including sleep (7 hours), then productive for financial (10 hours), consumptive (3.5 hours), and approximately (3.5 for transition or other) to total 24 hours of the day. Weekends would be heavily weighted to consumptive for this normal adult.

An average day for a working adult might look like this:

- **5:00 am to 6:00 am**—Wake and workout (productive for health)
- **6:00 am to 6:30 am**—Shower (productive to help get presentable to do a job for financial)
- **6:30 am to 7:00 am**—Breakfast with family (productive in building relationships)
- **7:00 am to 7:50 am**—Commute to work (productive if listening to a book on audible, consumptive if listening to music, or transition if neither of the other two)
- **8:00 am to noon**—Work (productive for financial with possible education and the possibility of consumptive or destructive, if the full four hours are not used to be productive)
- **12:00 pm to 1:00 pm**—Lunch (productive and consumptive if eating (health) and talking with friends at work (consumptive))
- **1:00 pm to 5:00 pm**—Work (productive for financial with possible education and the possibility of consumptive

or destructive, if the full four hours are not used to be productive)
- **5:00 pm to 6:00 pm**—Commute from work to home (productive if listening to a book on audible, consumptive if listening to music, or transition if neither of the other two)
- **6:00 pm to 7:30 pm**—Dinner (productive for health and relationship possibly)
- **7:30 pm to 10:00 pm**—Watching TV (consumptive)
- **10:00 pm to 5:00 am**—Sleep (productive for health).

## FINAL THOUGHT

Set goals to live your dream life, which is how you want to live each day. Then make plans and set milestone goals to reach this dream life. You can still enjoy life now while working toward the dream. But if you do not have a dream life or dream days, then you will have to settle for whatever you are given. You will have to then live for instant rewards.

Increase your awareness of your own productive versus consumptive and destructive habits.

My goal was to work hard for fifteen years so that I could live any way that I wanted for the rest of my life and to reach this goal before I was too old to enjoy it. My challenge to you is to retire by age 30 or 35, then really have fun and get really wealthy doing what you love that makes you a lot of money in the process. Again, a lot of money is whatever makes you happy. It could be $50,000 a year or $50,000,000 a year. You will know what a "a lot of money" is for you. And that amount, just as goals, can also change over time!

What is important for us is that we have self-worth, pride in what we do, give value to others, are productive in life, and understand that wealth is a mindset.

##  CHALLENGE TO YOU

TIME IS THE MOST IMPORTANT resource you have. Track your current weekly investment of time in a notebook or device, hour by hour. At the end of the week, calculate the percentages of productive, consumptive, and destructive time. Don't worry about making changes yet, the purpose is to practice awareness. Do this for several weeks. If you're at or close to 50% productive time, great! If you're not, later on, you can think about adding one more productive activity to your day or week to move the needle to the proportion that you want. The same goes for being too productive and if you need more downtime or consumptive time.

The most important thing in your late teens and early 20s is increasing your awareness of these concepts, so by age 25 or so, you can step on the gas for your productive 15-year stretch. Track your activities over time to increase your conscious choices.

# PART 3
## Apply it to Life

# 8

# ENJOYMENT

What is joy to you?

We have brief situations in life that give us what I'll call ultimate joy and it's the greatest feeling in the world—"the highest high." Think of some things that have happened to result in this type of joy for yourself.

For me, they are getting a great grade on a test or exam, winning a baseball game where my contributions made a big impact, graduating high school, getting married, my kids' births, buying our first home, and sleeping in that first home for the first time, getting a job, and starting a business.

There are also those times when we suffer brief (and sometimes not so brief) situations that result in the most devastating, depressive state of being. For me, they were fights with my dad, nights he kicked us out of the house and we had to sleep in a hotel or at my grandad's because mom did not have enough money for a hotel room, game losses where my lack of contribution affected the game's outcome, loss of a grandparent, failed test, failed college class, fights and breakups with Mom, not making it in the music industry, and closing businesses.

We all live on a spectrum of joy and unhappiness every minute of every hour of every day of our lives. We all have highs and lows, but hopefully, live within a more stable place on the spectrum. Each of us lives with a certain stabilized "joy factor," which I define on a scale from -100 to 100+ -- my totally unscientific, self-defined scale.

To a good extent, we can control the level of joy we live in daily, and even hourly. In the middle of the "joy spectrum," we cross the mid-line that turns to unhappiness, and at the extreme end, we have depression and despair.

## THE JOY SPECTRUM & YOUR STABILIZED JOY FACTOR

THE MOST ENCOURAGING ASPECT OF understanding the spectrum is knowing that we can control, to an extent, where we live on the spectrum. Sure, we will always have ups and downs, but planning and goals can give us more opportunities to have a plethora of highs and minimize the lows throughout life. It can also change our stabilized position on the spectrum.

My definition of joy is a positive mental attitude that is a direct result of my decisions through plans and goals. It's also a direct result of my *lack of* decisions, plans, and goals. Joy is something that I strive to be at the highest level all of the time.

On a scale of -100 to +100 "joy factor," which I made up as a tool to help gauge where I'm at, -100 equates to great depression or despair and +100 is the highest of highs of joy. My stabilized joy factor is probably around +65. I feel that I have felt ultimate joys at around +90/+95ish and have been lucky to only feel the ultimate lows from aforementioned life situations around -45/-50. I will say that at the time, I probably felt that I was at a lot lower factor (-95/-99 feeling).

Consider what you would want your stabilized joy factor to be between -100 and +100. Also, consider what have been the highs and lows for you and what positive and negative numbers would you assign to those situations.

Is there a difference between joy and happiness? I would argue, yes. Joy is an inner feeling. Happiness is an outward expression. Joy endures hardships and trials and connects with purpose. Happiness is dependent on external circumstances and is fleeting.

## JOY, GUARANTEED

THE WONDERFUL THING ABOUT JOY is that we have complete control over our level of joy. With the possible exception of mental health diagnoses, we all land on the "joy spectrum" by the choices that we make and the life that we lead. Just like making plans and goals will help you achieve success in life and the lack of planning and goals will result in the life society forces on you, your joy can have the same result from the same active planning and goals or the lack of planning and goals.

This is no different than the phrase "failing to plan is planning to fail." We have to take control and plan! A huge part of keeping joy is understanding that bad things do happen—they're unavoidable. The thing to do is to use those bad things as learning experiences. How we view and find ways to make bad situations better can give you joy while contemplating and harping on the bad situation will keep you in a negative state of mind.

Joy has a direct correlation with productive and consumptive time spent during a school day and weekend day. Additionally, the time spent on consumptive activities can be controlled and planned for greater joy. Not making a conscious decision on how to spend your time will default to a negative effect on your joy.

Sitting out in the sun or inside in the window reading an inspiring book would have a different effect on one's spirit than say lying in bed, curtains drawn, watching three episodes of Criminal Minds, Dexter, or hundreds of other dark shows. Watching a documentary might be more uplifting than flipping through social media and seeing all the negativity.

Additionally, forming a habit of lying in bed and watching most things that can be found on devices in my opinion is a destructive habit. So, please consider your consumptive time. Is the consumptive time utilized to give you a break and recharge you or is it going overboard and getting into unhealthy or destructive waters?

On top of the type of things you are doing during the consumptive time, it is very important to understand how much you can control that time and get both consumptive (breaks) and productivity out of this time. Reading non-school but fun educational books or listening to audible can take a consumptive hour to a productive hour. Going for a walk instead of lying in bed or on the couch also swings the pendulum for that time period, as well as enhancing your joy factor.

## JOY + SPIRITUALITY

Believing in a higher power plays a huge role in the long-term joy in my life. The freedom that I receive from having and practicing these beliefs is enormous.

My faith teaches that the two most important things one can do are to one, love God, and two, love all others. Forgiveness is probably one of the biggest ways to decrease stress and receive joy. It does take reminders to do this as I am human and it can be easy to hold grudges and bitterness. It is easy for anyone to realize and understand that holding hate in one's heart has no effect on the person who is the object of that hate but has an infinite effect on the joy of the person holding the hate.

Faith and spiritual practices encourage us to come together and worship. Church gives me personally and us as a family the opportunity to reset weekly as well as put things into perspective. Just listening to a pastor's understanding and view of how the Bible relates to things going on in our lives helps me to minimize or dismiss things that have been bothering me. Additionally, the singing part of worship in the church also gives a release. It is hard to be unhappy when singing at any time.

I truly believe if one attends church regularly with an open heart and mind, it allows the opportunity to clear stress and bring new joy. One final thought, this is a perfect time for family to be together. If nothing else is accomplished, attending church as a family and going to lunch afterward, is a great time for us as a family to renew and reset together and joy will follow.

## DAILY JOY RESET

As noted previously, there will be outside people and situations—joy vampires—that rob you of joy. As I have gotten older, I have come to understand and be more thoughtful of those who are trying to rob the joy from me. The phrase "hurt people, hurt people" comes to mind.

If someone is short with me and I do not really know them that well, I usually try to think about the fact that chances are that they are not upset with me, but with something else that has happened to them that day. If it's someone I know, I will even try to talk to them, if I think they are open to talking or let them be if I feel they are not in a mood for discussion.

We like to think those around us are in the same position in life. Unfortunately, many have troubled home lives, financial burdens, illness, mental health issues, and so many other issues. We have to be conscious of that.

## TWO JOY STRATEGIES

Two things I learned as a teen or young adult that I have depended on and utilized an infinite number of times through the years to keep joy and not allow stress to rob the joy are 1) put my situation into perspective and 2) when something feels overwhelming, to break it into pieces/sections/small hurdles instead of worrying about it or trying to overcome it in its entirety.

When I get "my feelings on my shoulders" or feel down about something, I have made a habit of always putting my situation into perspective by thinking about those who are in a worse circumstance than myself. I could make a list all day long about these circumstances, but the big ones that hit me are; children and adults with terrible sicknesses and many with "life sentences," all those in a hospital or those who need to be in a hospital, those who have lost loved ones in their immediate family or close to them recently (a parent, sibling, child, boyfriend, or girlfriend), those who have lost a job and cannot afford food for their family and the kids who feel shame around friends and do not want friends to know that they have had no food and are hungry, those who live with a handicap, those that live in an abusive situation, or live in a broken home or have a terrible home life, etc. When I consider all of these awful situations, my situation seems to feel much smaller or a bit easier to overcome. Even those who are in these listed situations can find people worse off than them. I feel and pray for those people in these terrible situations, and I think consciously about how I will use my many blessings to do better and help others.

## BREAKING IT DOWN TO ACTIONABLE TASKS

WHEN I AM OVERWHELMED WITH a job or a bleak outlook on a situation, I have gotten really good about taking the situation and breaking it into as many workable or doable parts. I have done this thousands of times throughout my life. In my experience, one of the biggest roadblocks for so many people achieving success is their inability to fend off stress.

Many times, the difference in overcoming or fending off stress is the ability to break down a situation and put it into perspective. Starting a new business from scratch might be a good example. Most consider the brainpower needed, the time requirement, all the different risks (risk of failing, risk of not enough customers or clients, risk of losing financially, risk of time away from loved ones, etc.), all the tasks and time needed to get a business opened, the unknowns, how the service or product will be viewed by friends and customers/clients, and many more to be too daunting.

Then there are the actual jobs of forming an entity, setting up tax IDs, registering through the state, local, and federal, articles of organization, partnership agreements, purchase agreements, real estate agreements, operating agreements, buildout plans, contracts with builders, equipment orders, bank loans, supplies, staffing, logos, credit accounts, marketing and so much more just to get one business off the ground.

I have formed more than 65 businesses or entities, bought some, started some from scratch, sold some, and even closed some that didn't make it. The way I have done this and have the capacity for hundreds more is through a recipe that includes business plans, projections, proformas, goals, plans, and timelines.

After taking the time to complete this recipe, things tend to be much easier and attainable. These items in the recipe help to break all the worries and concerns into small bite-size pieces that I am comfortable handling. Most people do not take the step of breaking down a big goal or starting a business. Rather, they look at the whole and say that is too much work, stress, and trouble for me.

Timeline is also a game changer here. Thinking about accomplishing these tasks altogether is overwhelming for anyone. On the flip side, breaking them down to tasks that take 30 minutes or an hour over six months makes it all doable, and achievable.

## JOY THIEVES—INCLUDING OURSELVES

EARLIER IN LIFE, I THOUGHT I was confident and I was, but not confident enough to get out of my comfort zone or worry about doing something others would perceive and think differently of me. There were so many times as a younger person when I let "not" getting invited to a party affect me that I actually did not hang out with the group that was at the party.

I had a temper as a kid and as I grew into a teen, I believe that it changed into a situation where I would not show my anger but I would let it live in me for a period of time. Because I did not have a way to vent my feelings whether anger or hurt feelings, I would bottle it up for up to two or three days. This is exactly what I mean by joy thief that only affected my joy.

When I talk about being mad (frustration or anger), I was very strong-willed and opinionated, which led to arguments with friends. It also probably kept me from getting invited to things from time to time like a group of friends going out or maybe even a party or two. Again, I would let the anger, frustration, or hurt feelings hold my attention for too long.

It took recognizing that those that I was angry with or had hurt feelings from did not think anything about it within moments of whatever was said. They got right over it. One day I came to the realization that I was affected, but they weren't. If they got over it and didn't care minutes later, why was I carrying it for a long period of time? After understanding it, I learned to just get over it. It was nothing worth anyone being concerned about. It also took having the thought of forgiving and forgetting.

My being upset did not have any bearing on them and their joy, just my joy. Some of this change was probably just growing up, but I wish I could have made these changes or grown up in respect to this a bit earlier in life and enjoyed life more possibly than I did. I believe that truly understanding and using forgiveness can be a life-changing decision and play a major role in Joy. I have learned how and have made a decision to forgive anyone and anything that has had a negative impact on my life. This is a much deeper conversation to be had, but in its simplest form, I have come to the understanding that a particular person did not hurt or harm me. Instead, their life situation and outside forces that they may or may not have control over had some if not all to do with what that person said or did to me. Understanding and accepting that it was most likely not that person's decision, but a position they were in which dictated how they acted. In this context, I can forgive all.

## HOW TO RESET JOY

If there is any advice that I could give on resetting joy it would be:

1) De-escalate the seriousness. It's hard to just say, "Don't take life and things so seriously," and even harder to do so. Ask yourself "Will this matter at all five years from now? Will I care or will anyone care about the thing I am upset about in a month?"
2) When you wake up in the morning, make a point to put yesterday's problems or issues in the past. Today is a new day.
3) When all else fails, sing a song. It is impossible to be pissed off or even frown while singing a favorite song. This can be done quietly in your room or as loud as you can sing while driving down the road. This has helped me so many times in life.

   I grew up loving different kinds of music. Pop and country during my younger years, but then I was a teen in the late eighties and early nineties (in my opinion was the best music ever made). I was listening to and singing, hair rock (Bon Jovi, Def Leppard, Motley Crue, Poison, and that list goes on and on), pop (Prince, Michael Jackson, Whitney Houston, and much more), and in between like Journey, Toto, and Huey Lewis and The News.

   To give the extremes I had some of the early rap like Run-D.M.C. to the Bee Gees, to Barbara Streisand, to the Everly Brothers, to the Carpenters. I could be caught at that time singing just about any song you can think of that was a hit in the late 70s, 80s, and early 90s, and can still be caught singing to all of those plus many of today's hits now.

4) Go for a ride (bike, train, car) and clear your head.

5) One other trick I use is no matter what is going on in my life, I think about being told that I have one day to live and I have to decide if I will let the issue or problem take my joy, which is taking valuable time away from me and my loved ones right then. For me, it always changes my perspective on the problem.

Finally, realize that unhappiness and happiness or joy usually grow one way or another. If you are unhappy and negative and show it, then you will most likely get unhappiness and negativity from the world, which will continue to feed that unhappy mountain that you are building. Or just the opposite can happen for happiness and joy.

So, the smartest and best thing you can do, as soon as you realize or are told that you are unhappy or negative, is to find a way to smile. Find a way to be positive. This is the quickest way that you will bring joy back into your day.

## 📍 CHALLENGE TO YOU

ASSESS YOUR PERSONAL AVERAGE ON the joy spectrum. Is it where you want it to be? What joyful activities could you add if you wanted to increase your number?

# GUIDANCE FOR DIFFERENT LIFE STAGES

My ultimate goal is to live in abundance, continually work toward the five wealths, and enjoy life to the fullest. And I want the same for you. I want you to enjoy life and everything you do from school, college, and your work—every day.

I hope that you wake up every morning and find something to feel thankful for and happy about.

## LIVE LIFE HELPING AND DOING FOR OTHERS

There are times that I forget this, but I realize that I'm much happier helping and doing for others. We are not here to make a bunch of money and die lonely. There is a fine line between being a good steward of what you've been given and trying to accumulate a bunch of stuff.

Accumulation of money and stuff will not make you happy. Doing for others through giving, helping, or providing jobs will make you happy. I love buying businesses and real estate, which are ways to make money, but I do it for sport and to have money to eventually give or do for others.

## DO NOT GET CAUGHT UP IN "STUFF"

IF YOU CAN AVOID THE allure of being better than someone else or showing off, it's very freeing. I have always looked up to Sam Walton, the owner of Walmart. At the time when he was the richest person in the world, he wore blue jeans and drove an old pickup truck.

As a kid, you may want to show off your "drip," but hopefully, you grow up and understand that it is only people trying to prove something that feels the need to flaunt their stuff. Yes, there are rich rappers, rock stars, athletes, and celebrities who want to show their "bling," and buy expensive cars, homes, jewelry, etc., but those people are often using newfound money to show off. They may be rich in cash or credit but oftentimes have a poor mindset. We can only hope that changes for them before it's too late.

## MIND YOUR CASH FLOW

KEEP CASH FLOW IN MIND before spending any money on anything, including investments. The time to be able to spend money for me is when I invest everything I can into an asset. That asset can be a rental house, a second business, a commercial property, or worst case for me would be the stock market (which is my lowest return on investment). So, to clarify, the money I made from the business where I actually worked from day to day, I used to pay for the basic needs and I invested everything else into an asset. I only use money made from assets to use as "spending money."

For me and for those who read this, I hope that they can do as I do now. I don't have money from actual work, as I don't have a job. So all of my money comes from assets. Now I use a small portion of that money for my day-to-day life and every extra dollar made goes into another asset. Those assets make money and that money compounds and grows exponentially to where they just keep growing assets and profits over and over.

Most money gurus will tell you to have six months of living expenses in cash, so if you lose your job, you could cover costs for six months, which gives you time to get back on your feet. This is great advice. I would work toward one year instead of the six-month mark and realize that living within your means on consumptive spending makes it much easier to set aside one year of expenses.

There have been three or four times in my life when I have spent two weeks to two years with sleepless nights unsure whether I could pay all the bills. I did not have enough cash set aside but instead used most of it for 20% down on a property or on some investment. It was money well spent and eventually helped me to make a lot more money, but that would not matter if I were not able to pay bills or if banks were to call with foreclosures or bankruptcy. I have skated by on all accounts, but keeping a good store of cash would have made life much easier for me.

Banks protect themselves by requiring their clients to invest 20 to 25 percent into a property or business. This gives them a cushion to be able to sell the property or business with a 20 to 25 percent loss, yet not lose money themselves if they foreclose on the loan because bills could not be paid to them.

Banks also require that the client retain at least 10% liquidity on larger loans. They want us to have liquidity, which is money that can be accessed at any time (this includes savings or checking accounts, the cash value in a life insurance policy, cash in a safe, etc.). The bank wants to make sure if things go south, we have time to right the situation, and the 10% liquidity gives a little cushion. I say that you should do this all the time without the bank forcing it.

For spenders, this is hard to do. I am a spender. Any money burns a hole in my pocket. I just happen to spend it on productive things—most of the time—instead of consumptive or destructive things.

As you begin investing more money, it becomes even more important to have 10% of liquidity of all debt. This means if you have $10,000,000 in debt (loans to a bank or mortgage company), then you should have $1,000,000 in liquid assets.

I've heard it said a million times that money magnifies who you are, which is a very true statement. So, when I say I am a spender, then having money just makes me want to spend more. I have to work to keep the 10% liquid. I am bad about dipping into that liquidity for the next investment, so my advice would be to hold yourself accountable and do better than me. It will keep the stress level down in your life.

## MONEY MINDSET

THE MAGIC MAXIMUM NUMBER TO spend on a mortgage or rent is 25% of your income. That is the big one. The biggest advice on saving that I can give is to never get into the habit of spending money before you get it.

Most people have in mind what they will spend their next paycheck on before they get the paycheck. Some are worse and spend it on a credit card before they get paid, then at some point get to where they miss paying it off at the end of the month, which quickly becomes a full credit card that they cannot make a payment on when they get paid. Don't get into that trap.

More importantly, when most get a raise or a new job, they quickly increase their spending to that level of income. The next time you get a raise or get another job making more money, then begin the process of paying yourself first. This means setting up direct deposit from your employer to your checking account. Then set up a second account or a savings account. Ask your employer if they can split pay you and pay 90% to your main account and 10% to your second account. If they cannot or will not, then have your bank help you set up an auto transfer to transfer 10% from your main account to your second account the day after the paycheck goes into your main account.

For those who don't have the money to save or are getting behind in debt with a credit card: get a second job. It is easy to deliver pizzas, become an Uber or Lyft driver, sack groceries, or do anything to help you get ahead.

The goal is not to budget, scrimp, and save, but to increase your income. And the ultimate goal is to get out of budgeting altogether. One of my definitions for financial independence is the ability to think of anything you might need on a daily basis, click on Amazon, and order it without even looking at the price. This is also the same for eating out.

You are financially independent when you stop looking at prices on a menu no matter where you are eating. It is embarrassing to say, but Amazon, FedEx, and UPS pull up to our house daily and sometimes multiple times a day. I honestly have no idea what any utility bill might be that we receive. I remember what it was like to be concerned about prices, bills, and the cost of any item I might need. I am very thankful for the freedom I have now by not having to be concerned with those costs. I hope that everyone who reads this book can have that freedom someday.

## QUESTIONS TO ASK AT DIFFERENT STAGES OF LIFE

First, I am proud of you and all the things that I know you will accomplish in life. As a parent, your joy and happiness are what give me the most joy. Now let's look at specific stages of life and note things that I want you to know for each stage.

## AS A TEENAGER

Up until this point in life, it has been hard to think of anything outside of yourself and how anything affects your world. It seems like everything is magnified as a teen which is most likely blamed on hormones. You will look back and think of your teenage years as some of the best times and some of the worst times in your life.

Looking back on myself, I can tell you that the positives and joys you have as a teen, you will remember for the rest of your life. "First times" are amazing and unforgettable. First boyfriend/girlfriend, the first time you went to the mall without parents, the first time you held hands, first car, first kiss, first beer or drink, the first trip without a parent, first day in each grade, first time to college, first college party, and the list goes on. There will be successes in life that will give you the same amount if not more joy than all of these firsts.

I am also very excited to tell you that the negative things will not seem as bad as you grow older. A breakup with your boyfriend/girlfriend that is so terrible now, will not be as devastating in the future. It is worth noting, that it will be up to you to figure out that you hold the key to your happiness, which means that you take in and enjoy the exciting times, accomplishments, and wins. At the same time, you let go of the bad things and learn from the mistakes. You get over it and do not let it eat you alive. The sooner you figure this out the better your life will be.

As parents we set rules and we make decisions that sometimes do not allow you to do some things as a child and as a teen. All of our decisions were made to teach and/or keep you safe. As you become an older teen, we begin letting go of the reigns and allow you to transition into adulthood, which means freedom. This is the greatest feeling for you, but the scariest for us. This is the greatest chance of you getting hurt or something bad happening to you. We say have fun but be careful a lot. As a teen, you cannot always make the right decisions.

We can only ask or beg you to think about the things you are doing and try not to put yourself in a situation where you can get hurt. Do not do things to be cool for others' sake, but do things that you want to do for yourself. You know this, but drinking or drugs multiply the possibility of bad decisions or bad things happening. So, be cautious of alcohol, and please stay away from drugs. Both are destructive activities and are rampant in high school and college. The consequences can have lasting effects if not deadly effects. I did drink in college but can say that I never did anything more than drinking (no drugs). I can also say that I never drank to a point that I was out of control or could not remember what I did while drinking at any time as a senior in high school, throughout college, and since.

## KINDNESS AND INTEGRITY

ON A LIGHTER NOTE, BUT just as important, get a head start in life by building up your integrity and treating others kindly. I will not go into a long rant here but just know that lying will never help anything in the long run. It may help temporarily, but it will be worse down the road. My advice is to be truthful or not say anything at all. If you are in trouble, let those around you know that you need to talk to a parent before saying anything else (this is especially true with police), but more importantly, do not get in a situation where you need to consider lying.

The second part of this was treating others kindly. Do not say or do things that will hurt others. This is true for face-to-face situations, but what is more important to consider is social media. Do not say or do anything on social media that you would not want that person, that person's parents, or your parents to see. If you even think it might be close to questionable, then just do not say or do it.

## AS A COLLEGE STUDENT

GET TO KNOW AS MANY people as possible. Build your relationship wealth. In addition to meeting as many people as possible, develop a few of those relationships. Do not just look for someone you enjoy talking to, which is important, but make sure that they have the qualities that you admire. You are an average of your four closest friends.

Also, remember that up to this point in life, you have spent the majority of your time on consumptive and hopefully not, but maybe even destructive activities. During college, part of having fun is making the most out of consumptive activities and unfortunately the possibility of destructive activities. Just remember that going to class is a productive activity that is working to improve mental wealth, so do not let the enjoyment of consumptive and destructive activities hinder productive activities. Working out for health is productive. Generally speaking, building strong future relationships is also productive. *Note, I am not condoning destructive activities, but acknowledge it because of what I saw in college. Instead of condoning, I am 100% against destructive activities. Remember that consumptive is having a drink, which becomes destructive if it becomes addictive or is abused by having multiple drinks at a time.

This is a time in life when spiritual wealth takes a hit for most teens. This is a perfect example of consumptive and destructive activities (partying on Saturday nights) hindering productive activity (church on Sunday mornings). I am not trying to shame you with this. It would be hypocritical for me to do so. I probably attended church five to ten percent of the time that I was in college than before or after college. I will just say consider doing better than me. It will reset you for the week and make you feel better.

## IN YOUR 20s

THIS WILL BE A WONDERFUL time in your life. Many more firsts happen in these years, especially with your own money. First job, first house, first car, first and hopefully only marriage, possibly first child, and more. Appreciate and enjoy these firsts!

My biggest piece of advice here, if you pursue marriage and a family, is 1) make sure you are in love and become best friends before getting married and 2) if at all possible, spend five to ten years with your spouse before starting a family. After children come into the picture, everything else takes a back seat. There is nothing better than raising children, but be selfish and enjoy some time with a spouse before having and raising those children.

## AS A PARENT TO YOUNG KIDS

ENJOY TEACHING AND PARENTING YOUR kids. While doing so, my advice is to set aside time for yourself and date times for you and your spouse. Do not become a parenting hermit. There is no doubt that your social life will lag the first three to five years of each child you have. Try to minimize this "social hit" by planning time for yourself and your spouse. You cannot give 100% of yourself to your children if you do not take care of yourself and your marriage. Additionally, you must love yourself and your marriage first.

## AS A PARENT OF TEENAGERS

THERE WILL BE MANY TRIALS and tribulations. You will be a great parent, but you will make mistakes. Do not be too hard on yourself when you make parenting mistakes. Know that your kids will learn more from your actions than your verbal advice. I think the hardest part of parenting for me has been when you have perceived something I have said or done in a different way from what I thought I was teaching, saying, or showing. This book series is a way for me to clarify my background and thinking. It is your responsibility to decide what if anything I am writing needs to be taken and used by yourself. Hopefully, you will use some of my points to stir thoughts and form your own opinions about life and the world we live in, as well as, how you want to live your life.

I would love to give you additional stages, but I have not "gone to school" on these future stages myself as of yet.

## ◉ CHALLENGE TO YOU

As with throughout the book, the challenge to you is to consider your mindset, don't be in a hurry, and focus on what you're already doing well. Building your wealth and becoming an increasingly conscious decision-maker is not a cut-and-dry, black-and-white scenario, but rather a process of growth. Practice observing what you're doing well, and when you're ready, build on that.

# 10

# DAD RANT

It's very easy to get caught up in what society holds as treasures. We want to reward ourselves for making enough money or reaching a goal in life. I do not believe it is wrong to buy something nice for yourself every once in a while.

The issue is that it is very easy to get on track to where that becomes the norm. If you realize that no earthly possession or person will fill a void or make you whole, but that giving to others and using treasures that you have obtained to help promote love or do good for others, it is then you who will be fulfilled.

My outlook toward life is to be as successful as possible and make as much money as possible to do great things. I want to give great amounts of money to help others through what I do with my money and success. I have struggled over many years with the thought of giving what I have now that will be divided and not go as far, as opposed to holding on to my money and using it to grow more money.

After much contemplation and calculation, I will be able to give more over my lifetime by doing the latter—making more money and creating more passive income streams first. I believe in giving extra to employees in need, those with little, those who are sick, and those who cannot help themselves. I feel that most of our taxes are misappropriated and should be used to give to those who are less fortunate (housing projects, food stamps, etc.), but so much more is needed for the less fortunate instead of needless government spending.

Our society continues to move away from faith and love. Society worships earthly possessions. Society holds celebrities to this high, almost godly, position. Society wants us to have what celebrities have and what our neighbors have. It promotes the following of network media, politicians, and social media without question or concern. Marketing rules. If we're not careful, as a society, we'll become zombie-like or puppets that follow along without even thinking.

It really boils down to laziness and ignorance. It is easier to not think and just do. It is impossible to understand things when one is not willing to think. I am talking about a society of consumers. More and more of our society becomes consumers every day. This is also why our society is in debt both at an individual and a national level. In addition to national debt, we also have states that are in great debt.

## WHAT MAKES ME PROUD

IT IS EASY FOR ADULTS to tell their children that they are proud of how they performed. Yes, parents are proud of how children perform in a sport, a play, or an event. They are proud of their school work and grades. They are proud when a child does something for someone else. I am always proud of you for those things as well.

It's hard to comprehend the feeling of being proud of a child. I believe there are times that the reasons for being proud are misunderstood by the child, which is usually the parents' fault. What I mean, as an example, if a child makes an "A" on a test or report card or plays really well in a game or sport and a parent says "I am proud of you," then it is sometimes perceived as the parent is not proud the other times the "A" is not made or an exceptional game is not played. A parent being proud is like a parent's love, which is unconditional. I am proud to be your dad and nothing can take that away.

Doing something wrong, something that hurts someone else, something that is immoral, something that is illegal, or even lying can hurt trust and can diminish the feeling of pride at the time, but does not change the fact or outweigh the proud feeling of being the parent of such a unique and outstanding individual that you are. So, as parents, maybe we should not say a specific action makes us proud, but instead, say that it makes us exceptionally proud.

For me, I want to clarify that I am first unconditionally proud of everything you do and for being the parent of a special individual. We might not agree on how we view things or how we do things, but that does not change the fact that I am proud of you. I do not care about grades or how one performs in an athletic event as much as I do about how hard you worked toward a goal and how you treat others in the process. So, I want to note a few other specifics of when I am proud.

I am proud when you show your independence and show leadership. As you get older, you will learn that leadership is not projecting your thoughts on others and trying to convince them that you are correct, but listening and forming your own opinion without stating your opinions or truths. Leadership is more about doing and not saying.

Your perceptions are not the same as everyone's perceptions. We are all different and have different thoughts and perceptions. You hear me say all the time "It is not just about what you do or say, but it is how it is perceived or misperceived." We all have different perceptions of ourselves and one another. As a parent, I am concerned about what you did or said to a friend that was perceived, not only by the friend but also by their parents. Of course, it could be misperceived by the parent, friend, or both.

Growing up with no money, without a parent or parents, or growing up in a different part of town/state/country can give one a totally different perspective than one who grew up with the money, two parents, or somewhere else. So, consider how your actions and words might be perceived by those who are not just like you and respect their views and thoughts. You do not have to agree or understand them but be respectful.

- I am proud when you learn new things. This could be an activity or simply the act of growing up and understanding new aspects of life.
- I am proud when I see you be the bigger person and let things slide.

- I am proud when you show that you can take negative actions or words from others and not let them affect your happiness and joy.
- I am proud when I see you bring happiness and joy to others around you with a kind action or kind word.
- I am proud of who you are and the great things that you will accomplish. I know that you will do great things. It might not feel like you will accomplish big things right now. Actually, I can assure you that there are many times that it will not feel like you are close to accomplishing things or being great. It might be years before you realize an accomplishment or recognize past accomplishments. However, it will happen. I know it and I am proud knowing it will happen. It is worth noting that accomplishing success or reaching a goal, while it feels great at the time, you will find that the process and the work you put in to reach this goal or accomplishment is most rewarding.

Really what I'm saying is that you should not waste your time being concerned with "Am I making my parents proud?" You have already accomplished that task. So, instead, enjoy setting goals and enjoy the act of striving toward the goals. A parent is most happy when they see that a child is happy. So, remember that life is about love and joy. Make sure throughout life that you set goals and attain milestones, but more importantly, make sure you enjoy "the ride" along the way.

Mom and I realize you are not our clones. Do not compare yourself to either of us. You will do much better than us in different aspects of life. The last thing that I want to do is to make you feel that I am setting this bar for you. I have lofty aspirations for myself. I am providing some instruction on how to attain wealth in different aspects of life. I am not setting any expectations for you. I have been blessed with a desire and drive to want to accomplish many lofty goals in life. Most people do not have these types of desires.

Additionally, I am not saying that it is better to be a follower of society versus someone who breaks convention or has lofty goals and ambitions over no goals. One can be truly wealthy in all aspects of life with their financial wealth being an income of $30,000 per year. It is a personal preference and more about living a full abundant life with love and joy. I grew up with less, and now I want more.

Money, however, when viewed and used in the wrong way, can make a person miserable. You get to determine what true wealth is in all aspects of your life. I will have failed with this book series if your takeaway is that you will never accomplish the things I have accomplished. Again, I am giving examples to show you that goals are attainable, but you set your own goals and the level of those goals you would like to attain.

## POLITICS AND MEDIA

I FIND IT HARD TO have a proper opinion on these groups without a moral and/or Christian basis. Our founding fathers, those that built our governing structure were religious and moral people and they began this country with a basis in Christianity. This means that the goals of the Constitution, Declaration of Independence, formation of Congress, etc. were grounded in doing what was morally correct. They wrote our founding documents and had a vision of a future government that was based on truth. Over time the purity of all of these foundations of truth that were used to form our government and politics has slowly been corrupted.

Our society along with our congressmen, congresswomen, politicians on all levels, and news media has evolved and lost much of its moral footing. This includes both religious and non-religious groups. It has gotten ridiculously frustrating to listen to politicians and news media, due to the fact that our country's citizens cannot believe anything that is stated. Call it "spin" or flat-out lies, the truth tends to be absent.

It's sad that we have gotten to this state of dishonesty. I like trying to find answers and solve problems, so I would prefer to look at ways to fix our issues so that citizens get truths from our governing leaders and those media members who are supposed to be giving us news truthfully. I believe that there are very simple fixes to these huge problems.

Number one, the simple answer is to hold those who are less than truthful accountable. The hard part is how to hold those who are lying accountable and the consequences of lying.

Number two, government officials should not be paid an annual salary. Instead, there should be an allowance for travel to Washington, DC, and an allowance for room and board for six weeks a year. All business that needs to be done in person should be done within six weeks. With technology, there could be other meetings through virtual online meetings, if needed. If the positions of professional politicians are removed, decisions would be attained much quicker. These first two changes would take care of any dishonesty and would help to get people into office who truly want to help our society and not be in it to make a buck.

Finally, there has to be some type of control over what is happening with the removal of different views on media. Freedom of speech should be freedom of speech. All media outlets should also be required to have some type of oversight and be required to be either opinion or news. If the platform is recognized as news, they should be held accountable for dishonesty and held accountable for the removal of any info that cannot be proven as honest.

These are oversimplified fixes. However, in regard to these "fixes," I can assure you that none will ever take place. It is my opinion, that our politicians and news outlets have gotten too much control with the dishonesty to pull back and fix these issues.

Sorry for the doom and gloom, but that is just how I see it at this point. I do not let it bother me or worry me because there is nothing that I can do about it at this time. Unfortunately, it will be your generation or the next few generations who will have to deal with it. For you, preparing by being in a wealthy position is what I would work toward.

Being wealthy provides you with some potential opportunities that you wouldn't otherwise have. Being financially wealthy specifically will possibly provide you the opportunity to make a decision to stay and fight the fight or to potentially move within the country or out of the country while things are not going so well in your town, state, or country.

Outside of growing your five wealths, I do not see any need to worry about the potential issue of the future state of our society. For me, this has a lot to do with prioritizing spiritual wealth first. Because I am committed to my faith, for me, it is simple to live according to my morals and beliefs and accept what comes in our future. It allows me the freedom to not worry or concern myself with the potential destruction of our society. I can only pray that you receive the freedom that I have.

# DREAM SCHEDULE: INVESTING YOUR TIME

What would your dream day, week, month, or year look like? The answer can be as superficial or as deep as you'd like. I'd challenge you to break it down and go deep. Understanding that there is no wrong answer, and your answers will also change as you get older and as you grow in your wealth. Remember to dream big while being true to yourself and what you really want for yourself.

As a teen, my dream day probably would have been a day when school was out, but I had a high school baseball game where I hit two doubles, a triple, and a home run while pitching a no-hitter. Or in college, maybe a football Saturday with a great fraternity party. But if I was dreaming big, it would have been writing a country hit and making it as a country music star. A dream week and year might have been 7 times or 350 times the dream days I have noted. All of this is still very superficial, but pretty much what I would expect out of just about any teen.

The truth is, I am not sure that I ever thought about a dream day, week, or year, but simply had dreams.

As I grew older, I unknowingly began to have thoughts of dream days, weeks, and years. Every new year I could grow a deeper understanding and gain clarity for what a dream day to year would be for me. Now I feel that I get to live those.

I now understand that in order to reach this level, I had to cultivate true wealth in every aspect of life while living an abundant, productive, and positive lifestyle. All of this true wealth and living dreams go hand in hand.

Sure, there are negative things that happen. We live in an imperfect world, so there is no perfect, love-filled, joyous dream day, but a truly wealthy person does not let a negative issue have a negative impact on their day. They instead let it roll off their back and learn from it. They look for the good and turn their thoughts to the next dream they want to accomplish.

One quick note on opening one's mind and dreaming big or setting great goals. We can have dreams that push us to do better and grow. Those same dreams can be walls or hurdles that we build for ourselves, making it hard to grow. In other words, we set this goal that can act as a ceiling for us. There is not one thing wrong with a person having a dream of owning a single business one day. However, that one business is all they will have unless they set a new goal.

Perfectly fine for most, but I myself have noticed that when I've set goals higher, I've achieved more. Another example would be my setting a goal to run a half-marathon, which I did set and did attain many times. However, I never ran more than a half marathon and still feel like running much more than 13 miles is not good for my body and somewhat impossible for me. Then I read about a senior citizen who has completed a 52-mile mountain marathon. So, now I question why a half? Why not more? My point is that we may set goals that are actually unintentional ceilings. Considering this, I challenge myself to expand my thinking or set higher goals than 300 restaurants and 300 restaurant properties.

For starters, if I have 300 restaurants, consider all of the suppliers that I need. Could I not buy or build new supply companies and own the properties where they sit? Could I not buy a warehouse and manufacture my own merchandise or buy farms that produce the foods that I sell? Hooters began as a chicken wing-based restaurant but now has hotels and casinos. Hooters had at one time and might still have an airline. The great thing about dreams and goals is that they have no bounds.

## THINKING BIGGER

GRANT CARDONE, A REAL ESTATE investor and author who wrote multiple books including "The 10X Rule" and has a YouTube channel of the same name, promotes the message of multiplying goals by 10. He goes further to say that he multiplies everything he does by 10 to reach his 10X goal, meaning working ten times harder and longer than everyone else and so on. His main point is that we are usually capable of much more than what we set as goals, which in turn suggests that goals can be hurdles or roadblocks.

Kris Krohn, the author of "Have It All", is also a good example of how to think big and really grow businesses, real estate, and wealth exponentially. I, like Grant and Kris, do not have any limiting goals. Successfully attaining a goal gives me the fuel to multiply my goals and think even bigger each time. So, once again, I encourage you also to dream BIG!

## HOW THE FIVE WEALTHS FIT INTO JOY AND YOUR DREAM SCHEDULE

LETTING ANY OF THE FIVE wealths fall to the wayside is a quick and easy way to rob oneself of joy and your dream schedule simultaneously. We can set goals and make plans to increase each of these five wealths. The old adage "failing to plan is planning to fail" when it comes to the five wealths. I set goals and make plans for all of these on a daily, weekly, yearly, five-year, ten-year, and twenty-year basis. Just working towards these goals provides joy. Achieving levels on a path to these goals provides wealth.

Understanding how I can set goals and plan now would have been very beneficial to me as a teen in high school and in college. I worked during my later years of high school and in college and having a better planned schedule would have helped tremendously.

I could've prioritized my schedule to have much more consumptive (downtime) during high school and college and shorter periods of productive time would have been much more productive than what they were. It is important to enjoy not working as a teenager (if you don't have to work) or enjoying as much downtime as possible. At the same time, one major goal in life is to find something you enjoy and are passionate about as your "job," then it really isn't a job. Just as noted previously for other aspects of planning and goals, if you don't make it a priority and find the job that you enjoy, life will provide you with a job as a default and it will not necessarily be something that you enjoy.

## HOW DO YOU REALLY WANT TO SPEND YOUR TIME

AS A TEEN, THIS ANSWER is easy. I want to sleep until noon, lay around, and watch shows or social media most of the day while snacking on junk food. Then around 5:00, I will see what friends are doing tonight. At 6:30 I will take a shower then go out around 7:30 or 8:00. I will get home between midnight and 2:00 a.m. usually and start all over again tomorrow. That was my plan as a teen without social media and I doubt it has changed much over the years for you today.

Now, I will say that while that is what I wanted to possibly do, I did not have the opportunity to live those hours 90% of the time. I had baseball practice in the afternoons most of my high school years. There were even days during school that I would go to practice baseball before school began. I woke many mornings when not working or when school was out to go hunting or fishing. I had between two and four jobs at a time during high school and college.

Jobs included bussing tables at a catfish restaurant, working checkout at a gas station, mowing yards for residential customers and a local church, doing clean up and construction at an older gentleman's fixer-upper house, doing yard work and odd jobs for two different families in town, doing clean up and cutting fabric for a men's boxers factory, working two years of high school and one year of college at a local magazine printing factory where I held five different type jobs over the years, working at a bank as a courier and ATM re-filler, as a telemetry tech at a hospital, and running the production booth for an after school online class that was live and interactive at three different schools in our state.

This does not include yard work and chores required of me at home during high school. So, my work ethic and initiative were ingrained in me. My parents worked hard, so it was easy for me to mimic their work ethic as well. I am not noting this to say "Look at me and all I did," but to point out why I feel that I am successful. I believe that I would have been just as successful if I had not worked at all as a teen but postponed work until after college.

But I can tell you that seeing how hard menial labor was to work at a factory, working double shifts, working night shifts, and just seeing adults who worked these jobs their entire lives had a huge impact on my outlook as an adult.

I know that working as a teen made it easy for me to work hard right out of college. Again, I think I had the work ethic to be a hard worker without the teen workload but I am not 100% sure that I would.

## MY WORRY

I WORRY THAT MY AND your mom's success and getting to a point where we did not have to work hard as you were growing might make it harder for you to have a strong work ethic. In my observation, being a child from a wealthy household more often than not results in unmotivated kids who lack direction when they become adults. I will say however, that I believe that the bulk of those kids did not have any direction from their parents and definitely did not have any books written for them to explain the importance of a strong work ethic, setting goals, planning, and being successful.

Mom and I had pretty much retired at ages forty and forty-one when you were nine and twelve. I actually used to say I retired at age twenty-eight to be a stay-at-home dad, but then went back to working at age thirty and retired again at age forty-one and have been retired ever since.

I note this to say that each of you on any given day (or almost every day) would leave for school at 7:30 to see me heading off to exercise or doing something around the house in a t-shirt and shorts. You would later come home from school at 3:00 pm to see me sitting in a recliner and watching TV. Of course, you might not have realized that I was not actively watching TV, but instead had it as background noise as I worked on my laptop in my recliner.

The point being that I saw my parents leaving for work as early as 5:00 am and returning between 5:30 and 6:30 five days a week. As previously noted as a teen, I worked two to four jobs all year from mowing lawns to construction to a printing company while going to baseball practice seven days a week. My jobs were required for me to have any money that I wanted to spend.

Meanwhile, your experience was having two stay-at-home parents who looked as though they did not work. So, again my concern for your perception and how you might mimic a work ethic that you could not see might have some validity. So, please take this chapter in and understand what I am trying to instill right now. You have to be productive and take initiative and have the work ethic to get into the "successful playing field," then the goals and plans can get you the "home runs," "touchdowns," or "three-pointers" that will create great wealth in your life.

## PLAYING THE LONG GAME

GIVING YOU THIS BACKGROUND IS also a way for me to provide you with an example or roadmap for transitioning from a consumptive teen to a successful and wealthy productive adult. Playing the long game is the way to be successful. A great sports team or individual professional athlete is a great example. They work really hard and work out and practice intensely over a long period of time and then reap the benefits of that hard work with the success of wins.

Working for greater goals produces greater results, even if the great goals are not obtained. Two things along these lines that I have learned. First, at age 15, my Sunday School teacher taught me a valuable lesson, which was teaching others is the quickest and best way to learn.

I truly believe looking back that he was just lazy and did not want to teach so each week he would pick one of us to teach the next lesson on the following Sunday. By studying to teach a lesson I learned much more than sitting and listening to someone else teach a lesson. This then translated into learning the second big lesson.

The second big lesson is, that instead of working to have one great business, I would work at it with a plan to have multiples of that type of business and would work in a way that I was going to teach others how to run these multiple businesses, while I ran one or two myself.

This automatically set my goals higher than most. Even if I ended up with two or three businesses or maybe even just one business, that one business had a much greater chance for success, due to my lofty goals and plans for multiple businesses. I was studying to teach a lesson on business, instead of listening to someone try to teach me, therefore I learned much more and was much more successful as a result.

Set goals to live your dream life, which is how you want to live each day. Then make plans and set milestone goals to reach this dream life. You can still enjoy life now while working toward the dream. But if you do not have a dream life or dream days, then you will have to settle for whatever you are given. You will have to then live for instant rewards.

My goal was to work hard for ten to fifteen years so that I could live any way that I wanted for the rest of my life and to reach this goal before I was too old to enjoy it. My challenge to you is to retire by age 30 or 35, then really have fun and get really wealthy doing what you love that makes you a ton of money in the process. Again, a ton of money is whatever makes you happy. It could be $50,000 a year or $50,000,000 a year. You will know what a "ton of money" is for you. And that amount, just as goals, can also change over time.

# SAMPLE GOALS, PLANS, BUDGETS + REVERSE BUDGETS

I'VE ALWAYS HAD THE MINDSET that if anyone else can do it, then why can't I? Doing a home improvement project, building a house, pouring concrete, running new plumbing, and running new electricity were all things I decided to try and do in my teens and twenties. I felt like I was just as smart or smarter than most people already doing those jobs.

Today I don't do as many of those types of jobs because I don't have the time. In addition, I know that I won't be as quick and efficient as a professional, and I have the means to pay someone else. However, trying and doing those things in the early days helped me to feel more comfortable trying bigger things.

Setting goals and making plans is really what will get you over the top in accomplishing great things. At age twenty, I never would have planned to do the things I have done now. I knew that I could accomplish great things, but never set any goals to think that anything big was even possible. At age forty-seven,

I am amazed at the things I have done and I have goals that I still feel are not only possible but are attainable.

## THE DIFFERENTIATOR

The difference between those "who do" as opposed to those who talk about doing, think about doing, and dream about doing—is those who take the first step toward making it happen. There are so many people who have great ideas and great plans, but they will never take the necessary action to make it a reality. Most of the time they are too scared, nervous, or lazy. To be successful at anything, you must take the first step and then the next. If you break it down into small steps, it becomes very doable. Many people make the mistake and think of it as a whole and feel overwhelmed.

Know that most people do not want you to succeed. There are many different reasons, such as feeling inadequate due to you having a big idea. Others are jealous of someone succeeding.

Most people just feel that something cannot be accomplished because it seems too big of an obstacle or something that is too hard to tackle. Most of the time it boils down to laziness, although they do not even realize that it is laziness.

## WHAT'S POSSIBLE—ACCORDING TO ME

I am providing the following list to show what is possible. You can accomplish anything on this list and much more. This list is not me bragging nor should it be considered intimidating. It simply shows what is possible. Most of this list comes from teamwork with me and Mom. Remember, I was a "C" student in high school and college and had to go back and get six more hours to graduate. I left college as a senior down six hours. We also had debt when we got out of school.

The list is in order:

1) Managed two different clothing stores out of college.
2) Fully remodeled a house that was around one hundred years old, which included running new plumbing from the water main throughout the house and running new electricity throughout the house.
3) Built out and started two dental practices and a clothing store.
4) Bought a property in Florida and built a second home/rental house on that property.
5) Purchased four more dental practices.
6) Purchased a third home or rental house.
7) Built out and started another dental practice (#7) and opened an orthodontic practice in an old practice space.
8) Moved a practice to a new location.
9) Purchased two commercial buildings.
10) Sold all 8 dental practices.
11) Purchased a commercial building (#3).
12) Sold the Florida house.
13) Bought a medical practice.
14) Bought a commercial property.
15) Bought a 56-year-old iconic restaurant.
16) Bought an 850,000-square-foot warehouse with two partners.

17) Bought 4 dental practices and 4 commercial properties in a neighboring state.
18) Bought two fractional ownerships at a peak lodge in Colorado.
19) Bought 2 more dental practices and commercial buildings.
20) Bought 2 townhouses in a college town.
21) Sold 2 dental practices and commercial buildings.
22) Bought two ranches in Montana that we will build on and rent.
23) Bought out my two partners in the warehouse.
24) Closed 2 more dental practices and sold one commercial building.
25) Bought an ocean-view villa in the British Virgin Islands that we will rent.
26) Bought 2 Social Security administration buildings in different states.
27) Bought a 26,000-square-foot retail/office space building with two partners.
28) Am currently building out the second restaurant location that will be rebranded.
29) I wrote this book and intend on writing at least nine more.
30) I have designed, patented, and will be producing a customizable caddy and intend to create six to eight more products.
31) I am slowly writing songs and intend on writing a couple a year.
32) I work out at least 30 minutes a day and play the guitar 30 minutes a day for five days of the week.

All of this goes back to the five wealths and being wealthy as a whole. It takes a while to really get started. I felt like I was getting nowhere for seven years out of college. I have seen friends take up to 20 years to get going on owning businesses or properties. It was easier for us due to your mom being a dentist and us starting her first practice, which gave us money and enabled us to do other things. I have found the saying to be true: "It takes money to make money." But realize you can use other people's money to get started with a good business plan. If I was in my twenties with no money but a great business plan, I would look for mentors or other relationships to find someone who might be willing to front the money or cosign on a loan for a large portion of profits from the business. There are other ways and it may take longer than I wish, but persistence is key. I will give more details in Roadmap for Financial Wealth.

## MY GOALS NOW

As noted previously, my plan now is to have at minimum 300 properties, write ten or more books, plus 25 to 30 songs, and own two restaurant chains of 150 plus locations each in my lifetime. I also plan to get and keep defined muscles and be in great shape for the next 30 years, which takes regular workouts 5 days a week.

I give you this information to say that nothing can hold you back. However, our mindset and the willingness to take the first step is the difference between wanting and doing. You have to be able to take the first step and then you can take one step at a time until you have accomplished what was once considered a pipe dream to yourself.

When making lofty goals and plans, do not listen to the naysayers. There will be plenty of them. Remember that the reason there is the minority and the majority is due to a wealthy mindset and actually working toward goals. The majority do not understand it and do not want to understand. They are consumers and usually have a scarcity mindset to boot. The sad part of the majority is that they are usually not happy and are not really successful.

In their mind, getting a couple of raises every few years and getting to retirement is a success. Those who are not happy or not successful do not want their friends to be happier or more successful than them. This goes back to finding good friends because you will be the average of your friends. Friends should be happy with your successes. My point here is that they can and will hold you back if you listen to them. Do not listen to them.

One final note, if I have heard it said once, I have heard it said 100 times. Persistence is what it takes to accomplish great tasks and be successful. You will fail and that is ok. Be ready for it, learn from it, and then go conquer the goal.

## HOLD YOUR VISION, MAKE AN ACTION PLAN

VISUALIZING HELPS TO BRIDGE DREAMS to reality. Dream big. No limits. Regularly visualizing will help to hit your goals. Some consultants would recommend a visual board, where you put pictures of those goals that you want to attain, which you know that I have in my home office.

Dreams stay dreams unless you set goals and make plans to attain those dreams. After you dream your biggest dreams, and then set goals and timelines, you can make plans to hit these goals. I write business plans, which include timelines and projections. I now write new or update the last business plans every year.

My plans get so specific that I break down each of my days into plans. I try to make daily plans and plan out my hours and even minutes between one and two weeks out. In my Notes app on my iPhone, I keep daily scheduled plans up to two weeks but also schedule activities up to two months out. I have every day set up for one year out in these daily plans.

I am certain that I have achieved all that I have done and future things I want to accomplish, due to goals, business plans, projections, timelines, and daily plans.

While completing all of my business, real estate, mental, physical, spiritual, and relationship goals, I am having regular lunch meetings and going out to dinner with the family every night. I am also able to do work around the house and mow the lawn regularly. We travel four to eight weeks a year and enjoy events regularly, such as football games, hockey games, and concerts. I also watch a movie or TV show for an hour or two a day. I truly believe that I would not be able to do all of these things if I was not using my time efficiently by using daily, weekly, and monthly plans.

You can accomplish anything - you just have to dream up what you want and have the tools to achieve the goals. Taking the first step is 90 percent of reaching goals. You also have to want it.

## THE DETAIL YOU NEED

SO MUCH OF WHAT I am preaching here is setting goals and making plans. There should be no stretch of the imagination that I want you to look at planning for your future with examples of my planning. Remember that my plans are updated and changed almost quarterly, as I update my Personal Financial Statement. At the time of this writing, I have decided to shoot for the moon and build my net worth to over a billion dollars. One billion is a big round figure and just a fun financial goal. More importantly, I have noted that I want to get to a point where I live comfortably with a very high standard of living on 10% of my annual revenues. The other 90% I want to go to our family charitable foundation.

In order to reach these two goals, I have a plan in place to grow two chain restaurants. Outside of the current restaurants, this does not include any of the other investments or businesses that I currently have or plan to have in the future. I will grow each to 150 restaurants and this will provide me the opportunity to own the properties, so all in I would have 300 restaurants and 300 properties for these restaurants. Additionally, I will continue to add commercial and residential real estate, as well as investing in other investment opportunities. The following is a very basic layout for how I will reach over one billion net worth figure and will go into more detail in a follow-up book:

Averaged, the two restaurant chains will each give me $12,000 monthly or $144,000 annual profits.

Both chains' properties will each give me $4,000 monthly or $48,000 annual profits.

All 300 restaurants and properties will provide $57,600,000 annually.

I roughly planned that the properties would cost $1,500,000 each.

The building, buildout, equipment, supplies, and working capital will cost another $1,500,000 each. This is $300,000 of my own money invested in each of the properties and restaurants.

It will take 40 years to hit 300 restaurants.

If I then valued the restaurants at a 7.5 CAP rate, which is the return on the investment, they would be valued at $768,000,000.00.

The properties would all have different balances on the financed loans where some will be paid off and some will have just begun. Remember that I will finance $1,500,000 for each property and for simplification I will assume that I will owe an average of 50% on all loans or $750,000.00, which is $225,000,000 for all 300 properties. I will also assume that these properties will appreciate at 3% over time and I will reduce 50% of that appreciation, due again to the fact that some will not have appreciated as long as others. 40 years at 3% is 120%, so a $1,500,000 property now will be valued at $4,750,540 and 50% of that amount is $2,375,270. So, the value of the properties will be $2,375,270 minus $750,000 for a total of $1,625,270 on average. With 300 properties, that is a value of $487,581,000.

In 40 years, adding the values of the 300 restaurants and the 300 properties gives a total value of $1,255,581,000.00. This is restaurants and restaurant properties only and not including the projected $57,000,000 or more annual profits.

There is a ton of planning that must go into hitting these annual profits, and I do plan out the specifics based on conservative numbers as I've done here.

As for your future, the sky is the limit. You can do as much or as little as you want. Just do what makes you happy. My advice is if you want to work in the same type of investments as me, then if I were you, I would get a business degree, a law degree, a commercial real estate license, or a combination of two or all three.

Any of these would bring more value to what I do. At the same time, I do not have any of these and it can be done without any of these degrees or without any degree at all. I do love running numbers, working on potential deals with proformas, and projections. So take this into consideration, if this is something you might not like. But even then, you can do what I do with other strengths that I might not have.

## TWO SAMPLE BUSINESSES

INSTEAD OF WRITING MY OPINIONS and my "how-to's," I will give you two real-life examples of goals, plans, projecting, budgeting, and also show how to scale. The first example is starting a small business (lawn service) and then an example of what I have already started showing you, which is how I am currently setting a goal of $1B and plans to attain the goal from rough generalized planning. This is to get the big picture of what's possible.

## LAWN SERVICE BUSINESS

LET'S BEGIN WITH A LAWN service. I currently have a hard time finding lawn service companies, so there is plenty of potential business. However, as with any service business, even if there is a ton of competition, one can be successful by providing better service, better pricing for service, or both.

You have this wonderful opportunity due to the fact that we currently have (4) commercial properties and (2) residential properties in middle TN that have lawns. These 6 properties represent potential lawn service revenues of the warehouse at $30,000, medical office at $7,500, dental A office at $7,500, dental office B at $6,000, residential A at $12,000, and residential B at $2,000 annually for a total of $65,000 annual revenue. Consider what it would be like to do these 6 properties alone.

On the profit side, let us say you have expenses of $10,000, which would leave you a $55,000 profit. This amount is more than the average American household income, not individual, household! Now let's consider hours of work weekly when mowing commercial properties every other weekend and residential every 7 to 10 days. The warehouse is 20 hours, medical office 2 hours, dental A 2 hours, dental B 2 hours, residential A 4 hours, and residential B 2 hours for a total of 32 hours every two weeks or 16 hours a week.

This is very doable for one individual with the proper equipment. 16 hours a week for 7 months and then 4 hours a week for the remaining 5 months. This is 485 hours plus 87 hours for a total of 572 annual hours. The hourly pay is $55,000 divided by 572 hours for an average hourly pay rate of $96.15. This is professional-type pay!

Now, let's look at the financials and workload with adding employees. With one owner/worker and three employees, we would divide the hours by 4. This means that the weekly hours would go from 16 to 4. Financially, the owner could pay each worker $20 per hour for a weekly payout of $240 ($20 times 3 employees times 4 hours a week). $240 per week for 50 weeks is $12,000, leaving a $43,000 annual profit for the owner. To take it a little further, let us consider that the owner is making monthly revenue all year, but can employ the workers only 7 months of the year. This means that the payout is not 50 weeks, but 30 weeks. $240 times 30 weeks is $7,200, which gives the owner a $47,800 profit. Now the owner would continue to work 4 hours a week alone for the remaining 20 weeks (off-season for upkeep). This means that the owner is working total annual hours of 200 while making $47,800 or $239 per hour.

With workers helping, the owner has now cut his workload and hours to 1/4 or 25% of the load or hours doing it all alone. So, what if the owner doubled the properties, which doubles the work and pay? This would be working 400 while making $95,600.

Now consider that instead of doubling the owner's hours, he pays a lead worker $25 per hour for the extra 200 hours. He will have the additional payroll expense of $25 times 200 for a total of $5,000, so instead of making an extra $47,800, he is only making an extra $42,800 without working any more hours. This is 12 properties with a profit of $90,600.

Now let us say that the owner hires one more worker at $25 per hour to do his 200 hours for those first 6 properties. Now the owner is not working any actual mowing and his profits are $85,600. When the owner stops mowing, he can then spend 1 hour a week checking all the work and making sure the workers are doing a great job.

He could then spend another hour every week looking for more work and then doubling the properties that his company is mowing. By doubling his profits, the owner now makes $171,200 per year. This owner is now making enough that he could hire a supervisor to oversee all work four hours a week for $50 per hour, which is $10,000 per year. Now the owner is making $161,200 and not working at all.

This means that the owner can go to college or start a different company while making $161,200 a year. This amount of money would rank this owner in the top 18% of income earners in the country without working. It is worth noting here that the service industry business will require some attention from the owner to stay successful. It will depend on the supervisor on how much the owner will have to be involved.

I would plan to spend 2 to 4 hours a week in the business to keep it successful. This can be done from another state by phone most of the year, with maybe quarterly check-ins at all properties. The 2 to 4 hours a week is talking to the supervisor(s) and calling customers regularly to check on their assessment of how your business is performing for them.

A few more fun things to consider with this type of business.

1) you can have fun working with friends and making memories while making good money.
2) you can build a brand name with truck or trailer wraps and t-shirts for uniforms.
3) you can continue to grow the brand and business as large as you would like.
4) again, this business can be grown while you are at college or starting a totally different company.
5) you could expand this business into pool service, mulching service, window cleaning service, car detail service, and many more by using the same scalable strategy.

This lawn service business example gives you a bit on setting goals with projections and somewhat reverse budgeting to get to a final goal amount. You can see that if this example gets you to $160,000 a year but you want to make $1,600,000 annually, you would need to do 10 times this number of properties each year with the same basic budgets and plans in place. It is worth noting that a commercial business's lawns will most likely pay better and would allow every-other-week service as opposed to weekly service. If you can find these companies, you or your business would be working half as much for double the money.

## 30-YEAR BILLIONAIRE GAME PLAN

My current ultimate goal is to reach a net worth of over one billion dollars by age 80. At an earlier age, I want to live on

10% of my personal income and give away 90%, which will be accomplished through a family charitable foundation.

Some other milestones or successes that I want to achieve along the way include owning houses in Colorado, Montana, BVIs, Bahamas, Santorini, Italy, Monte Carlo, as well as, a vineyard in California and maybe a place in the Swiss Alps. Other items on my list are a collection of exotic cars for investment purposes. These cars will be purchased in order; 2004 Ferrari 360 Spyder, Chevy Corvette Z06, 2001 Dodge Viper, Lamborghini Aventador, McLaren Senna, Bugatti Veyron, Ferrari Enzo, Ford GT, and a Lamborghini Diablo SRV.

All of these will need to be housed in a new garage that can hold ten to twelve vehicles. Some of the plans and goals to attain this ultimate goal include owning 22 GSA (General Services Administration) for Social Security and other government buildings. Additionally, I want to start two restaurant chains each having 150 restaurants, and simultaneously own the properties for these restaurants.

Finally, I will continue to grow my commercial and residential real estate portfolio. Outside of these plans, I want to help you start one or two business ventures and possibly allow you to be involved in some of my businesses. I would also like to be able to transition to running the charitable foundation and ensure that the foundation and our legacy wealth will continue for many decades.

I want to specifically look at how this is virtually the opposite of how schools teach us to be successful and how reverse budgeting fits into this view. Good grades and being successful in school and college teach us that we can get a good job.

Anyone can be wealthy in life by having almost any job because there is not a specific amount of money that gives any particular person the feeling of wealth and enjoyment. For me, the financial peace of wealth could mean $300,000,000 or $1,000,000,000 net worth, but for someone else, it could be a multiple of that—or a fraction of that. It's different for everybody.

Having a job working for a company or another person and being a multi-millionaire is hard to obtain, although there are a few exceptions. Being a multi-millionaire, billionaire, or even a trillionaire usually can often only be attained by owning businesses and employing many smart college grads to help attain the millionaire or higher status.

The major difference is thinking short-term or long-term. Short-term thinking is getting good grades, getting into and graduating from a good college, to then getting a great job. Long-term thinking is deciding what you want later in life and then deciding how you can go attain those goals. This is essentially reverse budgeting. Deciding what you will want and need and then figuring out how you can afford those wants and needs.

I have heard it explained before that if at any time we want something expensive, we should come up with an investment or business that would afford that "something expensive" item. Consider that line of thinking. If he wanted a $200,000 car, then he would determine how long he was willing to wait to buy the car. Then he would go find a business that would provide him the income to hit $200,000 in his decided timeframe.

The example of my current ultimate goals hopefully gives you a good idea of setting goals, planning, and reverse budgeting.

Always remember that you can be happy and live wealthy in all aspects of life with a great job, however, if you want a wealthy life that includes a very rich lifestyle or just having the money to help change lives for some less fortunate than yourself, then you will need to own the companies instead of working for one of the companies.

I am not saying one is better than the other, just that you will need to decide what is best for you. I will also state again that some higher management positions can make you rich with less stress than ownership. It is about finding what is right for you.

# WHAT I WOULD DO NOW IF I WERE YOU

What would I do if I was starting over as a teenager or twenty-something? Man, if I knew then, what I know now, I could change the world. This might sound a bit dramatic, but seriously, I could be so much further ahead. At the same time, we don't succeed without failures. There are huge failures, losses, and negative things that have happened in my life that have brought me to where I am now. As one saying goes, "To get where I am now, I wouldn't change a thing." However, there are maybe a few things that I would have liked to have known instead of learning the hard way.

## DREAM

My best and easiest advice is to dream. If you could travel through time and see yourself and your accomplishments at a particular age, let's say 70, what would you want that 70-year-old you to tell you that they had accomplished? Would you want them to tell you that they live on the beach, on some island, they became financially independent at age 50 and had spent their last 20 years traveling for six months of the year and volunteered at a charitable foundation the other six months?

Would you want them to tell you that at age 45 they learned how to sail, bought a $2M sailboat, and sailed around the world or made enough money to travel to space on one of the new public spaceships? Would you want them to tell you that they became wealthy enough that they spend their time with billionaire friends trying to come up with the best ways they can donate their time and money to make some part of the world or some part of their city or state a better place? It is your dream and it can be anything.

After you find the dream that really is what you would like to attain one day, then it is a matter of determining how you can goal it out and plan it out to where it can become a reality. A point to consider is that most people have a hard time believing that they can achieve more than 10 times what they are currently doing. If you are just getting started it might take starting with a goal of around $100,000 or $500,000 in a timeframe, say 10 or 20 years. If you can attain $100,000 in 10 years, then it might seem more attainable to 10X in 10 more years, which is $1,000,000 by 20 years. 10X over the next 10 years is $10,000,000 by year 30 and so on.

## WIN THE LOTTERY FANTASY

Another tip that I have used is to dream about winning the lottery at $50,000,000. If you won $50,000,000 what would you do with that money? If your answer is ways that you would spend it, you have not read this book or need to reread this book. You are not ready to grow your wealth. Hint—your answer should be how you are going to invest it and then use the profits from the invested money to spend on something cool or do something good for someone or society. If you can dream about how you would handle winning the lottery, then you have your dream, now let's figure out how to goal it, plan it, and attain it.

## READ BOOKS BY WEALTH EXPERTS

I WISH THAT I READ books from Robert Kiyosaki, Dave Ramsey, and Garrett Gunderson, along with many others when I was in college. I could have saved a ton of time and really gotten a head start on growing wealth, even if not by taking action, but by learning how wealth is made. However, some things we must learn through life situations.

And to be fair to a teenage me and to be fair to you now, our minds are not willing and able to care about what these authors were and are teaching. I will attempt to give you now my perspective on what I would have liked to have known at 18, 20, 25, or even 30 years of age.

## FIND A WEALTH MENTOR AT 10X YOUR CURRENT INCOME

THE AGE OF THE MENTOR is not that important. What is important is the level of wealth of that mentor. A good rule of thumb is 10X here as well. If you make $100,000 per year, it will most likely be a waste of time to talk to someone worth $100M. They will be talking over your head. It is better to find someone making $1,000,000 per year to mentor you if you are making $100,000 per year.

When you reach $1,000,000 per year then find someone making $10M a year and so on. So, the goal would be to dream big and find a dream that you want to shoot for. Then, goal it out and put it on a timeline that doubles every 10 years or so at first. Then you can try to find a mentor to help you get to your first 10-year milestone goal. If you just cannot think that big, then set a shorter-term goal that is 10 times what you are doing now and find a mentor making around that goal to help you work toward that goal. When you reach that goal, go back through the process of trying to dream big or 10X it again, if not the big dream.

## CONTEMPLATE TIME MORE CLOSELY

NEXT, I WOULD REALIZE THAT time is the biggest and most important factor that influences my goals. It is also the one factor that I cannot control. There is NOTHING in this world that I cannot accomplish with time. I have heard people qualify this statement with "outside of physical restrictions." I've even used this phrase to qualify the statement. However, I have changed my thoughts on this qualifier.

I would now state that there is NOTHING in this world that I cannot accomplish with the proper amount of time. I am 5'11," which is somewhat "short" relatively speaking as it relates to football, baseball, and basketball players, yet you can Google "shortest NBA, NFL, or MLB players" and find professional athletes that are 5'7" or even shorter. So, persistence and drive still play the biggest role in anything one wants to do in life.

At one point, I wanted to be a singer/songwriter/artist. When it came down to it, I decided that the life of an "artist" would not be as important as having a normal life and family. I still believe, in my mid-forties, that if I really wanted it bad enough, I could fulfill my original dream of being an artist in country music.

I also wanted to be an optometrist when I was in college. I applied to an optometry school. I did not have the grades to get in and did not get in. I could not be happier now that I didn't succeed in this goal. However, I feel confident that I could be accepted and get a doctorate degree in optometry or even ophthalmology if I had the drive to do so now. What is the oldest age of an optometry school graduate? I read that a guy graduated at age 69 from one optometry school, not sure if he was the oldest, but it is possible. Again, not something that I want now, but definitely doable.

My point here is to never sell yourself short or take the easy way out by justifying that you are too old, too small, too whatever. You can do it! Time is the biggest factor that cannot be controlled. I have no doubt that I could die with a financial net worth of one hundred billion dollars, that is $100,000,000,000. What I am not sure of is that I could do it in the next thirty years. Maybe so, but maybe I need 50 or 100 more years to do it with good growth. Unfortunately, I do not see myself living to be 146 years old. I do not see myself living past 85 years old. So, again, time is an uncontrollable factor.

## UNDERSTAND THE LONG GAME

IN ADDITION TO CONTEMPLATING TIME, I would start thinking about the long-term goals for what I want to accomplish by age 60, 70, and 80. It is important here to realize that when setting goals, we do not paint ourselves into a corner. I have missed many goals. I have also reached many goals in much less time than I originally set for myself.

Look at it like this, if you begin taking a flight of steps up to the top floor in a one-hundred-floor skyscraper and you are only allowed five minutes to reach your top-floor destination, you might not make it to floor one hundred in the five minutes. However, you might make it to floor 50 or floor 20, which is much higher than floor one, where you were starting. Setting high goals that might be missed, can still produce great results that would not have been considered with no goals. The majority of people don't have goals and plans, so I would first set some lofty goals. It is also worth noting that people generally fail to hit short-term goals but actually overshoot their long-term goals.

## REVERSE BUDGET

NEXT, IF I WERE STARTING out at age 18 to 25 or younger, I would reverse budget, which would be to determine what I wanted to accomplish and then back into goals and plans to reach those accomplishments. I would also not put as much stress on myself to be successful right away. It takes time to be successful.

With long-term goals and planning, it makes it easier to plan out a timeframe for good growth. It might have taken me eight years to make $500,000, which I might sometimes make in less than a month currently (closing a deal). In sixteen years, I plan to make over $8,000,000 in a month (again, I will go into depth in Roadmap for Financial Wealth).

No, matter that figure, with the proper planning and investing it is possible for you to double your income over ten years. This would mean that you could potentially make $60,000 per year now and make $600,000 per year for the following 10 years, and so on. Saving is a bit harder, but let's set an attainable goal of saving $5,000 per year at first, which might have to be a second job.

The next ten years, maybe 10X that monthly figure. No matter, it takes time to get started. Consider working for free for the right mentor for a period of time. I would even make the bold statement to say that I feel that I could have been more successful working and mentoring for free under different mentors for four years than going to college.

## FIND YOUR PASSION

FINALLY, I WOULD MAKE SURE that I had time to determine what I wanted to do in life. You really will not know what you want, what you enjoy, or your true passion yet at this age. What is hard is wasting time growing in a direction that you ultimately will not be going in. What is your passion? Take a few years after high school or college to figure out what you really enjoy doing and then start working on it. The last thing you want to do is to spend 15 to 20 years in something that you wake up one day and realize you hate.

## FIGURE OUT WHAT YOU WANT IN LIFE

AS A TEENAGER, THIS IS a huge multipart question. I never had this type of question posed to me. However, if I were starting over as a teen, this would be a good question to ponder. Know that the answers to this question can and will change over time.

The best thing I know to do is to answer the question now as if I were a teen. Hopefully, this will spur thoughts for your answers. Don't be afraid to answer now and don't be afraid of change.

Here's my take on my teenage view: what I want out of life is freedom, an abundant life, to be wealthy in all aspects of life, and to grow in my Christian faith. As a teen, there is no concern for providing for myself or others, but I want to begin thinking about being able to provide for myself, a future spouse, and future kids. If I begin planning now, I have more time to reach all my goals. I need to build a foundation of a good education in the field that I feel that I want to be in, as well as, build great relationships with good people. I want to choose friends carefully.

I would consider doing a couple of internships over the summer in college or right after college. I would find a way to work for free for a couple of wealthy people that I look up to for two to three months, if not more. This would give me a great idea about what I want to do or quickly prove to myself that it is something that I do not want to do.

## KNOW YOU CAN CHANGE YOUR PATH ANY TIME

BY THE WAY, IF YOU do wake up in 20 years and find that you hate what you do, it is not the end of the world. Make the change and go into the new direction that you would feel better in. The worst thing that many find themselves doing is deciding that they are stuck in the life that they have created for themselves and they have to stay on that path forever. You DO NOT and should not live an unhappy or unfulfilling life, so make the change at any age, even 69 or 79 years of age.

Also while 18-25, enhance your financial education with books and conferences. I have and will continue to challenge you to read non-fiction books while in school and college. Even if you just read or listen to one during each summer, it will help you tremendously. Health is a wealth that is easy to concentrate and succeed at while working on and in the other wealths. Spirituality is an ongoing journey and getting ahead is better than waiting. Relationship is also one wealth that you can really succeed at while growing in financial, educational, and spiritual wealth in these years.

## CHOOSE YOUR FRIENDS WISELY

I WOULD FIND FRIENDS THAT are positive influences on me. I would think about the five wealths and make sure that I have friends that help or challenge me in those wealths. I would want to have friends who would influence me to grow in the Christian faith, work out and be healthy, challenge my mental capacity, make me want to succeed in whatever business or financial endeavors I am in, and help me to enrich all of my relationships. These can be different friends for each wealth or I might be lucky enough to find a friend or two that help in multiple wealths.

We are an average of our closest friends. Starting college and high school are great times to step out of friendships and into new friendships. Never burn bridges, but distance yourself from any negative friends in your life. Try to find those with abundant and wealthy mindsets. Even if you are in the middle of college or high school, you can transition carefully toward other people if need be.

All people have opinions and things they want to do. Do not try to dictate the opinions they should have or what you think they should do. It is ok if they are wrong, incorrect, or just different in their thinking. People do not like being told what to do. If you dictate opinions, then you will lose good friends and end up with whatever friends are left. These "leftover" friends that are ok with and will put up with being dictated to will most likely not be the friends that will help you grow.

It is important to have patience with friends and learn to listen and allow others to have a say. Additionally, know that people do not like hearing about you and me but would rather talk about or hear about themselves. It is fine to tell friends about things going on in your life and have great conversations about opinions on different topics, but make sure that more than fifty percent of your conversation is about them. Ask them questions about them. Let them talk about what they enjoy, like, and dislike. Again, you might not agree, but you do not have to make your disagreement known. Instead, change the subject and find something in common that you can agree on.

## YOUR SIGNIFICANT OTHER, IF YOU CHOOSE TO HAVE A SIGNIFICANT OTHER

Your mom and I have been envied by many friends over the years. We were lucky enough to find each other early on in life, become great friends, and build a great love around our friendship. I did not have the same feelings with any other people I dated as I did for your mom. I had a different level of respect for her.

So, I would want to find someone that I like and that likes me for who I am, who understands and gets me, and who wants the best for me in everything I do. I would want to feel the same for that person too.

Know that you will disagree, argue, and maybe even fight from time to time, but if you find the right person, you will be willing to bend and give for their needs and they will want to do the same for you. This may not be the situation at any given moment, but after each person has time to reflect, you both will want to work out any differences.

## PARENTS, TEACHERS & OTHERS

I would want to have a good relationship with my parents and feel comfortable talking to them and getting advice from them. I know that I had times when I did not want to be around my parents because I wanted my independence, but that time passed and I ended up feeling comfortable talking and getting opinions.

Know that we want to help you in any way possible. We have tried and failed at many things and are a wealth of knowledge of what not to do. Do not be afraid to ask!

Teachers and professors supposedly became teachers and professors to help others learn. I would view teachers and professors differently now versus how I did as a teen in that I would go to them, text, or message them and ask for help if I needed it. If they could not help, I would ask for suggestions on other help, such as a tutor. You will most likely gain some points just by asking. You will also get some great help hopefully!

School and the real world are very different. Be a sponge and learn all you can in school, then when you get out, you can apply what you learned and begin relearning in a new way to do things in the real world. The hope is that most of the things learned in school will be of some help. You will definitely learn life lessons in both high school and college.

## LEGACY

HAVING ALREADY HAD KIDS AND beginning legacies, it is fun to go back in time and think about what I would do or want to be done differently. I would want my kids to know they are loved, to know that anything I have said "no" to or upset them by not allowing them to do something was only meant to keep them safe or teach them something. I would want them to grow up with everything they could ever want, but treat others in a way that those others never knew that they had everything. I would want them to be kind, loving, forgiving, and have patience with others. I would want them to know that these qualities are much more important than knowing things or making money or being better than someone else. I would want them to know that being the smartest person in the room also means sometimes being the quietest person in the room. Show knowledge through actions, but do not feel that they have to prove knowledge with words.

I would want to have a relationship where the kids can come to me for any reason and know that I will not judge, but try to guide them. I would want them to not be scared or ashamed and know that I have made some of the same mistakes when I was their age. I want to be their best friend after they have grown and gotten out on their own. Up until then, I want to be more parental and teaching, therefore being a friend is not seen as easy for them, although I would love that.

I want to build a financial legacy for our family as well. We have properties in Colorado, Montana, the Bahamas, and the British Virgin Islands. These are properties that we want to stay in our families for generations. So, turning back time, what I want for my future kids is to provide long-term generational properties that will contribute to their families' enjoyment throughout their lives. In addition, I would want to create a legacy of great relationships and family where we come together and enjoy time together wherever we might be.

# APPLYING THE 5 WEALTHS IN YOUR TEENS & EARLY 20s

I WISH I HAD KNOWN and understood the five wealths much earlier in life. I might not have acted on it in high school or college, but I would have been introduced and could begin thinking with a different mindset. I did set many goals in different aspects of my life as a teen and young adult before being introduced to the five wealths, but had never put it all together as a whole.

As far as what I would not do, I would not miss out on understanding and working toward the five wealths as soon as possible in life. That is about it on the "would nots."

I want you to understand what wealth truly means and to move away from thinking you want money or possessions. I would want to have a mindset of true wealth in all aspects of life and to also have an abundant and producer mindset.

High school and college years are a time to enjoy life, have fun with friends, and learn who you are and what you want. There does not need or have to be much investment into the five wealths during this time. However, knowing and understanding the five wealths, along with abundance and a productive mindset, is a huge step that would get you ahead of everyone else.

I would start as a teen and set goals, make plans, and begin initiating some of these plans. I do a new business plan for my life and update it annually. This business plan is a plan you would see for a business, but it is tweaked to lay out goals, plans, timelines, and projections, for one's personal life instead of a particular business.

It obviously encompasses the five wealths with productive and abundant mindsets. This is a time when you can dream and dream big. It can be really fun to lay out a path on paper to where you want to go in life and how you want life to look and feel for yourself. I like to save a new draft every year and then update the draft with new goals and tweaks to old goals. I think it would be interesting and fun to look back and view one's life plans at the different stages of life and see what has and has not changed.

Understand that you do not have to have a perfectly laid out plan for life as a teen. You might not know what you want to do or to get out of life while you are a teen. If you do have the perfect plan, it can and most likely will change. A plan as a teen would be more about specific short-term goals (6 to 12 months). Any long-term goals could be 3 to 5 years. 10 to 20 to 30 years out could be the dreams if you get to the long-term goals at all. Remember that they need to be specific to each of the five wealths.

If I were a teen now and knowing what I know, my plan would look something like this:

**Spiritual wealth**—Short-term would be attending church as regularly as possible, listening to the New Testament for five minutes a day four days a week, and spending five minutes when I wake up praying or meditating and reflecting on the weekdays. The long-term would be to know I could be more regularly attending church and to really increase my time praying as well as reading or listening after college.

**Health wealth**—Short-term would be to eat healthy during the week and indulge on the weekends a little, do some type of exercise with a friend or alone for 30 minutes three days a week, and most importantly be careful with my alcohol intake while in college or just don't drink at all.

Long-term would be knowing that eating healthy and working out is a long process to get into shape and stay in shape if you want to keep it up and make the small life changes. I would re-evaluate the next year and maybe make more specific long-term goals.

**Relationship wealth**—Short-term, I would want to realize that college can be the time that I have the biggest opportunity to meet new people. It is where I can build up the courage to step out and make introductions. Get to know people. Find those with like interests and good values (good people) and become friends with them. Most of the people I meet I will not become best friends with, but I know that the more people I meet and make an acquaintance with during college lends the better chance that I have a connection with someone later in life for personal or business needs.

I would set a goal to meet someone new every day I have a class at school. Just reaching out and introducing myself and being nice to someone will give me a great positive feeling for the day. Also, I would find a way to compliment them if I could, which can also be the easiest way to start an introduction. I would also make conscious efforts daily to not talk too much, but instead, ask questions and listen (without giving my opinion), while agreeing and letting them tell their story.

Long-term I would plan to find three to five close friends that I have made throughout college and then have as many acquaintances as possible (100, 200, 500?). Consider that if I attend college five days a week for around 36 weeks a year, that is 180 new people met if I meet one a day. And over four years, that is 720 people.

**Educational wealth**—Well heck, I'm in college, so what else do I need to increase my mental capacity? I would say that reading non-fiction books is somewhat of a way to "be friends" with someone. If someone smart or successful in any of the five wealths writes a book about what they know and what they have learned, then that is a great way for me to get to know that person and in turn, I will make my life more like them just by learning from them. So, I would set a goal to read or listen to two or three non-fiction books every year. I currently listen to some of the same books year after year. Outside of this, learning a musical instrument or writing my own book is a way to increase mental wealth. Long-term I would build on my mental wealth and make sure I keep it up over the years.

**Financial wealth**—In college, not a ton of ways for me to make money working an hourly job. I would consider these four years a time for me to invest in myself to be financially successful in the future. I would look at entrepreneurship, starting a business, designing or inventing a product, and/or writing a book for my income instead of working an hourly or salary job after graduating college.

I would then research and find ways to give myself a better opportunity to be successful as an entrepreneur, a new business owner, a designer or inventor of a product, a writer of a book, or many other avenues. I would start while in college or I could prepare and be ready to go hard as soon as I graduated college. Long-term I would have a goal to start a business, be an entrepreneur, writer, etc. by age 25 or three to four years out of college. A lofty goal, but that would be my goal and I know that I would need to begin thoughts and preparations during college.

## MAKE A DAILY PLAN

I SUGGEST HAVING A DAILY Plan for the five wealths. Make it the first five minutes of your day praying and reflecting, the next five minutes listening to the Bible, and the next five to ten minutes planning out your schedule for the day (but knowing it can change in college). Find 30 minutes to work out three days a week, probably right after my first twenty minutes of spiritual time.

Plan your day to include 15 to 30 minutes of listening to a non-fiction book and 30 minutes of thinking about plans for your future and a path to financial wealth (this can include dreaming big time). Finally, plan to compliment and meet someone new for that day. This hits all five wealths and will not take up much of your day. Taking weekly or monthly breaks from this is good also.

It does not take much time daily for personal or business planning, but it will make a huge difference in each day and in life overall. It is not as much about time spent daily, but persistence and making a habit of it for life. Finally, much of the time in college can be easily wasted. Focus on finding a way to be more productive than consumptive or destructive. Try to spend more than fifty percent of your time being productive and doing something that helps one of the five wealths.

## DON'T WAIT FOR A LIGHTNING BOLT

I WISH I COULD TELL you that things suddenly "clicked" for me at the age of 26, and that's why I'm so sure you can start your own sprint then, but I can't. It was really more over a five-year period around that time when I really began to understand how the world works. This was the time I grew up and began making adult decisions.

I began to see what planning would do and started setting goals that set me on the path that I'm on today. I wouldn't change my life and the things that led to my success in all aspects of life, but I will say this: if I had changed my mindset and my way of thinking at age 18 or 20, to what I'm conveying in this book, then I would be six to eight years ahead in business compared to where I'm at now.

Let's say that I am successful in doubling my wealth every five to seven years. That would mean that whatever number I achieve when I stop growing businesses, which will be my death as far as I'm concerned, means that I would have doubled whatever amount that ends up being. As someone, at a certain age and stage, committed to giving 90% of my passive income away to charitable causes, for people in need, and for entities that can do good—that matters.

What you do now matters.

# SUMMARY

As a parent, I have spent my last sixteen and nineteen years teaching you, as my children, all of the things any parent tries to teach their kids. Those things are: what to and not to do, right from wrong, how to stay safe, how to eat well, be courteous to others, tell the truth, make good grades, how to crawl, walk, run, ride a bike, and hundreds of other things. Many things you have learned not from what I have said, but from how I act. Some of these actions are good and a few unfortunately not so good. I hope you have figured out that I am not perfect. I make mistakes and I am continually learning. You will do the same throughout your life.

Something that changed my way of thinking from my youth to adulthood was the understanding that I did not know everything. I now realize that I know very little and that helps me to be open to ideas and growth. I have found that those who think they know everything tend to be the more ignorant in our society. Learn not to talk, but to listen in all social settings. You will quickly understand who among those talking are smart and who are not. Back to my point, although the last sixteen and nineteen years of my life have been dedicated to teaching you the basics of life and how to live as an adult, I wanted to give you something that would teach you more about the rest of your life, and your future.

This is planned as the first in a series of books of things I want you to know or things I wish I knew as a young adult starting out. Most of this is about mindset and perception. You have a good chance of being able to understand and use these teachings because you are my children. Most of society ("the 99%ers") could read and maybe understand this book, but could not put these teachings to use. I should say that anyone could put these teachings to work if they decided to take the steps and be persistent. However, it is like those who go on a diet year after year with no real results as opposed to the few who change their way of living to get the results they want to achieve. The 99%ers will keep trying the diets, but the 1%ers (and hopefully you) will know how to make changes to their lifestyle that will give them and you the results. If you feel you fit into the 99%ers group and are happy, there is nothing wrong with that. The fact of the matter is that most would prefer not to take the steps required and that is why our society is made of those ninety-nine percent of people. If you want to "change teams", I am hoping this book has provided the playbook for you.

It is important that you use what I am giving you here to help make your own decisions. You will possibly disagree on some of the topics and that is ok. This is not a right or wrong series but instead meant to be information to help you as you grow. I can assure you that I will change my mind on some of my thinking in this book over the next few years. A perfect example is that in this book I wrote about doing what you love.

A few weeks later I read about someone else's thoughts on the idea of doing what you love as a job, which he felt was total bull. My personal perception was that I am lucky to do what I love and I do believe that those who are truly wealthy do what they love as their jobs, but now know that there are some who are wealthy that do not love what they do. A better way to put it might be to work toward what you are passionate about. Or better, work to accomplish what you are passionate about. It takes hard work and maybe doing something that you do not enjoy for a period of time, to get to a financial position to do what you are passionate about.

Personally, I am passionate about growing all wealths including financial wealth. I am so passionate about growing wealth, that I actually enjoy doing things that I might not enjoy otherwise. But in actuality for myself, I love growing and setting goals. I love trying new things, new businesses, new ways to make money, and attaining goals that I have set for myself in all five wealths. Therefore, I am in a unique position and blessed to do what I love and am passionate about.

I worked from 15 years old to 40 years old doing whatever it took to be successful, then was able to retire (financially free) and able to then do what I love. So, take this into consideration, when I say do what you love or what you are passionate about. Remember also, that neither I nor anyone else dictates what makes you happy or what you consider successful. You determine your happiness and success. While my definition of success is being wealthy in all aspects of life, there are those who feel that becoming a professional athlete is the pinnacle of success. Others set a high IQ or being one of the most knowledgeable and smart people in the world is the highest aim, while others feel that going into a business field or healthcare and becoming the top of their field will do it for them. Furthermore, others feel that teaching students or helping those in need is an ultimate success. Any of these are perfectly fine, as long as that is what you set for your personal success. You are the driver with this Roadmap in hand, you have the ingredients, and it is your decision now to make the fifteen-year sprint!

# EPILOGUE

In the period from writing my first draft to publishing this book, almost eighteen months have passed. When my daughter read a very early draft, she was 18 years old and a freshman in college. During her sophomore year, she called one day and said, "I'm not getting the value out of these college courses, it's a waste of your money." The idea of investing tens of thousands, actually a couple hundred thousand on this education wasn't tracking for her. "I have learned more working with you in a couple of weeks this past summer than I have in a year and a half here in college."

Mom begins asking questions, "Are you having trouble in classes? What are your grades like?" Her response was, "No trouble, grades are good, I am just bored and realize I am not learning anything that I feel will be utilized in the real world. Working in the businesses this past summer was fun and exciting and I am wanting more of a challenge. Dad, you mentioned something about a dog boarding facility close to school."

This was the point where I realized that she had been paying attention. I'd seen a posting of a boarding facility that had good profitability and was sitting on 12 acres of land. It was being sold with the business and the building. My daughter has always loved dogs and all animals. She had considered being a veterinarian in middle school. "Yes, I will check and see if it is still available. I think the numbers looked pretty good", I said.

I found the business listing and the return on investment was in my acceptable range. We structured the deal in a way that we put $8,000 down and the annual profits would be $90,000, which is a 1,125% Return on Investment. The seller was an absentee owner, meaning that he really was not involved in the day-to-day, which would be a great business for her to "cut her teeth on." In addition, they were not selling any products and doing no marketing. We quickly decided that conservatively, she should be able to increase profits to over $100,000 within the first year or two.

A week after we decided to purchase the business, she called again. She had been discussing marriage and her future with her 3-year boyfriend. "We want to buy a farm back in our hometown, but it will be so much more expensive in three or four more years. Would you and mom consider buying a farm now for us?" she asked.

"I understand and appreciate that you want to save the appreciation by purchasing now, but we are talking about around a $3,500,000 property at current pricing for what you are asking about. I never write a check for a deal. I use the bank for leverage, which means that I need to find a way to pay the monthly note. This means that I would need to make money through rent or other income. You would not have a way to cover that debt." I said.

This was an opening for another great educational opportunity. I went on to talk to her about reverse budgeting, goals, and plans for buying the farm herself. With an average salary for what her boyfriend's degree would provide and her annual income of $100,000, they were still a long way from a $3,500,000 farm. However, I showed her that owning five more of the same type of boarding facility with similar profits would indeed get her what she wanted. "But Dad, that will take years and we want to own a farm in three or four years," she said with a deflated tone.

I quickly let her know that she could do it in three years. She asked, "How"? And I explained that it is possible to buy one boarding facility that is five times bigger with five times more profit in one purchase. I also let her know that it could be done with three more purchases in the next three years. I could tell that it was a "lightbulb" moment for her.

A month and a half into owning the business and she cannot be happier. She is quickly learning about running a business. I have made a point to have her handle everything. Mom and I are available and answer all questions, but she has to do the work. We had an interesting call a few weeks ago where she stated that she has never been on an interview, but was scheduling interviews with prospective new staff. "What do I need to ask them?" Was one question. "It's weird when I decide against an interview from a resume of college graduates when I have not graduated myself! I had a lady twice my age saying yes ma'am to me," she told us.

I should note that we are 50/50 partners in the business. She gets a management salary and then we split profits 50/50. But our deal is that I make my original investment of $8,000 back fourfold $32,000 (we rounded down to $30,000) and I would step out of the deal. Her next goal will be to buy into the property that the business leases. She will be able to buy in 50%, but I doubt I will sell the other half to her, as my goal is to never sell a property.

It has only been 45 to 50 days, so we will see where it all goes from here. She is still living at school, enjoying the extracurricular activities that college offers in a college town (fraternity parties with her boyfriend and sorority social events with her sorority sisters, etc.) I doubt she will go back to college. Mom and I are happy for her to go back or to never go back, as we understand that she has the understanding and mental capacity to be a great entrepreneur who needs no college education. She is getting what Robert Kiyosaki calls "a real education."

This experience has been a great example of what setting goals, reverse budgeting, and planning can do to reach that ultimate goal and will go a long way for her to reach her wealths. Consider that if she adds five more facilities with five times more profits, she could be sitting around $600,000 annual income in as little as three or four years. Of course, having her mom and my financial backing and guidance gives her a huge "leg up." Without our investments, maybe it takes her 14 or 15 years with traditional bank financing. But with her current plan in place and us on her team, she may just be at a point of my definition of retirement by age 23 or 25. Her 15-year sprint might be done in 3 or 4 years.

Most would stop there! I would push her to keep going and growing. She could easily be financially wealthy by age 25, but how does that impact her other wealths? Financial freedom and "retirement" from hands-on work then give her 40 to 60 hours a week (that most people are working at or in a job) to grow. Grow mentally through masterminds, reading books, underwriting deals, and more. Grow relationships with time to meet others that can help her grow in the different wealths, and have plenty of time for family and friends. Grow spiritually and physically by spending time alone and working out with others. And grow financially by researching and looking for bigger and better deals. Her possibilities are endless and so are anyone else's who has the mindset, thinks abundantly, is positive and joyful, sets goals, makes plans, and works to grow all aspects of wealth.

# ABOUT THE AUTHOR

Dee is an investor and entrepreneur. He currently owns or has previously owned businesses that include dental and medical practices, clothing stores, restaurants, construction, web, and app companies, a commercial landscape company, pet boarding facilities, and a commercial development company. In the dental space, he rolled up and sold 16 dental and ortho practices. He is most heavily invested in real estate with a very diverse portfolio of dental and medical buildings, warehouses, strip centers, government Social Security Administration buildings, restaurant and boarding facility properties, college student housing, and vacation and legacy properties in eight states and three countries. Other current works include a development in Abaco, Bahamas, a real estate management app "Property Pro", and Iconic Restaurant Group and properties. With over $100M in business and property assets, Dee is putting investment deals together to help build his restaurant group and restaurant properties to annual revenues of over $1B. He is currently writing "Roadmap to Wealth Series" with this being the first book in the series.

Dee and his wife, Sara, live in Franklin, TN, and have two wonderful teenage kids. This series was written specifically for his children as a way to pass on the true understanding of wealth. As a family, they enjoy traveling and spending time together. Dee and Sara have an ultimate goal to have their Charitable Foundation give away $90M annually.

www.ingramcontent.com/pod-product-compliance
Lightning Source LLC
Chambersburg PA
CBHW050334010526
44119CB00004B/141